# JACOB'S DREAM
## Setting Out on a Spiritual Journey

*Cardinal Carlo Maria Martini*
Archbishop of Milan

*Ron Lane*
Translator

*A Liturgical Press Book*

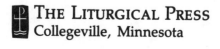
THE LITURGICAL PRESS
Collegeville, Minnesota

Cover design by Mary Jo Pauly.

*Il Sogno di Giacobbe* © copyright 1989 by Edizione Piemme S.p.A., Via del Car-mine 5, 15033 Casale Monferrato (AL), Italy.

| 1 | 2 | 3 | 4 | 5 | 6 | 7 | 8 | 9 |
|---|---|---|---|---|---|---|---|---|

**Library of Congress Cataloging-in-Publication Data**

Martini, Carlo M.
   [Sogno di Giacobbe.  English]
   Jacob's dream : setting out on a spiritual journey / Cardinal Carlo Maria Martini.
      p.   cm.
   Translation of: Sogno di Giacobbe.
   ISBN 0-8146-2000-0
   1. Youth sermons.  2. Catholic Church—Sermons.  3. Sermons, English—Translations from Italian.  4. Sermons, Italian—Translations into English. I. Title.
BX1756.Z8M3713  1992
252'.55—dc20

                                               92-7542
                                                 CIP

# Contents

# Introduction

## Preliminary remark

*Lord, we feel ourselves incapable of facing the mystery in the call to stand before you during this retreat. For this reason we ask you to allow the Spirit of the Covenant to speak in us, to speak in me, O Father, to speak within the heart of each one of us.*

*Make us live in intimate contact with the Holy Spirit that you, Father, have sent to us in the name of Jesus, your Son. We ask you to enliven our hearts during this time, enabling us to be led by that Spirit which was poured upon each of us at the time of our baptism and confirmation. Enliven our spirits in faithful union with this Spirit who rules and governs the entire Church of God. May we be in union with the Pope and the bishops, with those responsible for all the churches throughout the world, with all those governing in the Church who truly seek the kingdom of God.*

*We ask you to enliven us during these days with a sense of our communion with all the young men and women of our diocese, with all young people everywhere who are seeking the kingdom of your Son, and also with those—perhaps more numerous—who are not searching for the kingdom. We wish to be here not only for ourselves but for all missionaries, especially for those who suffer from persecution and those who have recently sacrificed their lives in missionary countries; for those Christians who are in prison on account of their faith; and for the many young people who because of their faith must endure all manner of hardships and sufferings. Finally, we ask you, O Father, simply to enliven these days in heartfelt union with young people throughout the world.*

By ourselves, we are not very capable of thinking great and holy thoughts. I cannot really tell you something deeply important, nor are any of you in a position to say something of deep and lasting truth and seriousness to the rest of us. Rather, our capacity comes from God, who, by the Holy Spirit, writes a living letter on the tablets of flesh in our hearts (cf. 2 Cor 3:5ff.).

*Understanding where I am* is the subject of our retreat. The phrase is particularly meaningful to the person who is traveling. When you change your location you need to re-orient and ask yourself, perhaps after a night spent on the train: where am I? how did I get here?

We need to understand where we are not only physically but above all spiritually, and especially when we are on the verge of making great life decisions. Then we experience the need to bring together the coordinates or points of reference in our existence and ask: where am I now? and why am I at this point?

This task of self understanding is called in the New Testament *discernment*. Essentially, it is a question of knowing the will of God, and it is this that we hope to become clearer about during the retreat.

Let us recall some passages of the New Testament where discernment is spoken of.

—*Romans* 12:1-2: "And now, brothers, I beg you through the mercy of God to offer your bodies as a living sacrifice, holy and acceptable to God, your spiritual worship. Do not conform yourselves to this age but be transformed by the renewal of your mind, so that you may judge what is God's will, what is good, pleasing, and perfect." We here today also want to discern the will of God, to know what is good, perfect, and pleasing to the Lord.

—*Philippians* 1:9-10: "My prayer is that your love may more and more abound, both in understanding and wealth of experience"—that is, in full understanding of what the will of God is for you—"so that with a clear conscience and blameless conduct you may learn to value the things that really matter, up to the very day of Christ."

—*Colossians* 1:9-10: "We have been praying for you unceasingly and asking that you may attain full knowledge of his will through perfect wisdom and spiritual insight. Then you will lead a life worthy of the Lord and pleasing to him in every way. You will multiply good works of every sort and grow in the knowledge of God."

### What I propose to you

The three passages from Saint Paul clearly indicate what we intend to do during these retreat days. Allow me to expand on this by telling you a) what I am proposing to you, b) in what way I desire to help you, and c) how you can help yourselves.

What I propose for you is the work of discernment, of trying to know the will of God in your life.

This is an exercise in attention, in listening to the Spirit of God in our soul in order to grasp the divine will in its direction of our life. Discernment is listening to the unwritten word of God, which even today resounds freshly and uniquely in the consciousness of all the faithful.

This unwritten word of God is a summons, and it is found in anyone to whom God speaks *here and now*. It is not in Scripture, nor is it known by any Church authority. Should I ask the Pope if he knows this word of God? Might my bishop be able to tell me what it is? No, this word of God is intended uniquely for me. Each of us has to seek this word or voice that calls within the confines of our own soul for our personal journey, a voice that no one else is able to hear for us.

I can, of course, seek advice from others about my life, but no one is able to hear *this* word for me. For here we are dealing with the mysterious dialog of God with me alone and in which I ought to welcome the unwritten word or words which admit of no substitution. And in this process discernment is a very important activity. Some people think that they can pick out, at random, a page of Sacred Scripture in order to understand what God is saying to them. Of course, it is true that whatever the Lord is saying generally to humankind through the Bible is valid also for the individual. But Scripture does not supply that utterly unique word I am seeking.

One does not usually hear this unique word in the daily round—though no doubt it can erupt even in instinctive and routine life (I eat, I drink, I amuse myself and, then, at some point I just might hear and advert to such a word). But as a general rule I recognize this particular word of God for me in a spiritual climate and activity, within the setting of the life of the Spirit, that life that we want to live more intensely during these days of the retreat.

How, then, does one know this word that tells me where I am? It's necessary to do three things:

1. to purify oneself interiorly from every sin and all the destructive thinking tied to sin;

2. to meditate on and contemplate God's world, the great framework of the plan of God of which I am a part. The elements of the divine plan are revealed to me first of all by Scripture and are mediated to me by the Church and its magisterium, by all that makes up the teaching of the faith;

3. to reflect on the whole of the elements of the divine plan in the framework of the various features of my personal life: historical, psychological, familial, affective, bodily, emotional, spiritual.

All this is involved in understanding exactly where I am. Within the confines of these three conditions I perceive the word of God for me.

In this meditation on our lives we will try to help ourselves by looking at the very dense experience that Jacob had, as recorded in the Old Testament, when he sought in the midst of his journey "to understand where I am." It was a dark moment in Jacob's life; but by opening to the mystery of God he came to understand where he was and to have a clear view of his situation.

As we read the biblical passage (Gen 28:10-22), we can see it as a symbol of our own endeavor to comprehend where we are.

### How I can help you

I have come to help you in this task of discernment because I believe you are living through an extremely important time in your life.

As I've already said, *I* cannot tell you what God's word for you is. But I can accompany you on your journey, sustain you amidst posssible fears and discomforts, in your hours of aridity, and when you are feeling somewhat lost.

I shall accompany you first of all by praying for you and for your unique life journey. Beyond that I shall guide our reflection by meditating on Jacob's dream. Finally, I shall listen to you, both in the group periods when you are sharing your thoughts and feelings about the faith and in personal conversations with you.

In all this I feel a single desire: that you live in the most authentic way possible the truth of your own life within the truth of God. Having gone through this search for God's word and will myself, I obviously bring my own personal experience to bear on what I say, as well as the experiences of many other persons whom I have known and known about. But my concern above all is to pray that God's will may be uniquely realized in each one of you.

### How you ought to help yourselves

Our meeting here unfolds in a climate of prayer, and you will help yourselves by actively participating in this spirit and initiating your own prayers.

I urge you to profit from this time by praying longer than usual. And I am thinking of your using the simpler forms of prayer: a decade of the rosary, brief ejaculatory prayers, periods of quiet adoration in the chapel. You may use traditional prayers as well as pray in your own words. And remember, we are here for the sake of all our brothers and sisters in Christ. I would like you in your prayer to recall the suffering, impoverished, marginalized persons in the world. Let us offer ourselves to God for the sake of those who live a crushing existence. And let us hope that one day we can help them even more so that they too will be able to live in a decent, human, and spiritual dignity.

You will also help yourselves by meditating on Scripture since it manifests God's world, the world of true reality, *the* world with which the ingredients of our life should be fundamentally coordinated.

Thirdly, you can help yourselves by writing down impressions, questions, reflections about what you are presently experiencing, what you are currently going through in your life. Writing gets us used to looking objectively at ourselves, frees us from the turmoil of our imagination and the confusion and disorder in our thoughts; it helps us to put our lives in order. Besides clarifying our mind and deepening our reflection, what we write down may become something we wish to talk over with another person.

I conclude this introductory section of the retreat by recommending two practical exercises to be done during our mornings here.

The first is to write down as precisely as possible your responses to the following questions: what do I want from these days, what do I hope will emerge? And, what do I fear may happen? Write this while placing yourself before God in words such as these: "Lord, I come before you. Help me as I ask myself what I really want, what I'm afraid of, how I would really like to go forth from this retreat."

The second is to pray a psalm while you are quietly in the chapel or walking in the garden. A very suitable one is Psalm 139, which begins with the words, ''O Lord, you have probed me and you know me; you know when I sit and when I stand. . . .'' Read it calmly. Try to place yourself within its meaning—perhaps with the help of any citations in the margins of the biblical text refering you to related Scripture passages. It will not be difficult for you to grasp some meaning from the psalm that bears upon what each of you is living *here and now*.

# Where Am I, Lord?

*We ask you, Father, through the death of your Son on the cross, to open our hearts to an understanding of your Word. Enable us not to be frightened of this new experience but to live it patiently, minute by minute, with the certainty that you are leading us even through moments of silence, aridity, weariness, and the feeling of abandonment, because you are greater than we are and our hearts find their rest only in you.*

After the excitement of the first hours of coming together here and beginning our retreat, we have now settled down enough to confront our fundamental meditation, the Scripture passage about Jacob's dream. We will try to respond, under the guidance of this biblical text, to the question: Where am I, Lord?

## Reading from Genesis 28:10-16

"Jacob departed from Beer-sheba," in the southern part of Palestine, "and proceeded toward Haran" (Gen 28:10). This was no little trip, for it meant travelling through the whole of Palestine, going into Syria and then into Mesopotamia, thus returning to the land from which long before Abraham had left in the beginnings of the history of his people. Jacob had to go a thousand miles on foot, a fearsome enough adventure.

"When he came upon a certain shrine, as the sun had already set, he stopped there for the night. Taking one of the stones at the shrine, he put it under his head and lay down to sleep at that spot" (Gen 28:11).

Reading this, we have the impression of a vagabond, a fugitive who doesn't have a suitable cloth to lay his head on and who falls asleep, exhausted, not really knowing where he is.

> Then he had a dream: a stairway rested on the ground, with its top reaching to the heavens; and God's messengers were going up and down on it. And there was the Lord standing beside him and saying: "I, the Lord, am the God of your forefather Abraham and the God of Isaac; the land on which you are lying I will give to you and your descendants. These shall be as plentiful as the dust of the earth, and through them you shall spread out east and west, north and south. In you and your descendants all the nations of the earth shall find blessing. Know that I am with you; I will protect you wherever you go, and bring you back to this land. I will never leave you until I have done what I promised you." When Jacob awoke from his sleep, he exclaimed, "Truly, the Lord is in this spot, although I did not know it!" (Gen 28:12-16)

We can divide the passage into its two principal parts: the *first part* shows us Jacob all alone; the *second part* shows Jacob, in the dream, with God.

It seems useful to me to identify these two parts with the aid of two questions: Where does Jacob think he is? Where, really, is he?

### Where Jacob thinks he is (vv. 10-11)

Geographically, as appears later in the episode, Jacob is at a place called Luz and which subsequently will be called Bethel (Beth = house; El = God). He is about three days' journey from his home, far enough away to feel that his past is somewhat behind him. Another month's journeying, however, will be required for him to reach his destination; and for this reason he feels himself completely lost, abandoned, deprived of reference points. Here we see the connection between geography and sociology: we cannot be at home in a physical place without the personal relationships that make it meaningful.

Some time before, Jacob had broken with his brother, and in effect with his family. He was extremely saddened because his behavior had caused serious consequences, as appears from the preceding chapter: ''Esau bore Jacob a grudge because of the blessing his father had given him. He said to himself, 'When the time of mourning for my father comes, I will kill my brother Jacob' '' (Gen 27:41). We see here another instance of that tragic conflict between brothers that constitutes much of the history of sinful humanity, beginning with Cain's fight with Abel, continuing through the discord between Joseph and his brothers and present today, for example, in the conflict between Arabs and Jews. Jacob himself was undergoing the suffering of a family broken in an almost irreparable manner by grave misunderstandings and contentions.

But there is more. In the present situation at Luz, Jacob does not have his mother's assistance and protection, such as he had enjoyed earlier. ''When Rebekah got news of what her older son Esau had in mind,'' that is, Esau was planning harm to his brother, ''she called her younger son Jacob and said to him: 'Listen! Your brother Esau intends to settle accounts with you by killing you. Therefore, son, do what I tell you: flee at once to my brother Laban in Haran, and stay with him a while until your brother's fury subsides and he forgets what you did to him. Then I will send for you and bring you back. Must I lose both of you in a single day?' '' (Gen 27:42-45).

His mother, no longer able to maintain peace between her sons, had to choose the lesser evil—itself a serious matter— and urged one of them to go far away.

Jacob is a man whose most intimate bonds have sadly been struck at—thus, he has had to abandon his father without so much as a good-bye. He has been compelled to separate himself from all his tangible points of reference.

Nor is he morally at peace. He seized his brother's inheritance by a subterfuge. He is an imposter, a supplanter (as his very name indicates), and he is unable to think of God protecting him. His sin troubles his conscience.

Financially, he has nothing, and without money he is trying to get away to safety.

In short, Jacob no longer has the three reference points that from the very beginning of biblical times have been constituitive of the human being: God, family and friends, land and work. He feels himself to be in some way cursed like Cain, and it is not by chance that Scripture represents him to us in the darkness of the night, alone, disconsolate, and with these questions burning in his heart: where am I? what will become of me?

Jacob feels himself to be in a condition in which he cannot depend upon anything in the future, either good or bad. He is an alienated, disconnected man, one who feels as though he is no longer really able to count on any definite reference points in his life.


### Where Jacob really is (vv. 12-16)

There appears now the extraordinary answer to the second part of the story, one which answers this question: Where is Jacob really?

In the dream the word of God reveals to him what are the *invisible* and nevertheless decisive coordinates or reference points of his life.

Let's divide the narrative into three parts, having to do with the symbol, God's proclamation, and the lasting promise.

1. The *symbol*: "Then he had a dream: a stairway rested on the ground, with its top reaching to the heavens; and God's messengers were going up and down on it" (v. 12). This symbol has been employed many times throughout history, and Jesus himself uses it when he says, "You shall see the sky

opened and the angels of God ascending and descending on the Son of Man'' (John 1:51). Many are the meanings that the Fathers and Doctors of the Church have attributed to Jacob's vision. St. Bernard, for example, sees the human being's relationship with God as a staircase on which one goes up and down.

What does this symbol really indicate? Simply: *God is interested in us.* In those situations in which we believe we are deprived of precise reference points there remains an absolute reference point in our life—that which we call Providence or the mysterious presence and action of God. This is the first fundamental revelation, bound up with the great attitude of Judaism, the holy fear of God. God mysteriously takes care of us human beings, never abandons us, not even in what appear as our darkest and most difficult times. In the dark night of a wandering and fugitive individual like Jacob, heaven is watching and monitoring his every move. We are the object of a Providence that follows us step by step even when we feel ourselves downhearted, disoriented, and desolate.

The fact of this providential care is the most fundamental truth, the most basic fixed point there is in re-establishing order in one's existence. It is not exclusively a Christian reference point, for it is there for every man and woman in the world who senses that life is not all calamity, misfortune, and toil— nor, for that matter, all good fortune, either. More significant than whether we experience good or bad luck, easy or hard times, is the fact that our life is ruled by something greater than us. This great sense of providence, present among peoples throughout the world, makes the human person religious, at least at a basic level.

God looks after me, I am in the hands of the Lord. All the persons who cross my life, all my sufferings (which I ought neither to curse nor minimize), are under this revelation that is the prime fixed reference point and focus of my life, a focus that I ought never to lose whatever may befall me, in whatever situation I come to find myself.

Jacob needed this certainty that, come what may, God was looking after him, taking care of him. And we, too, need this same assurance.

The opposite of such a recognition is thinking that existence is simply a mute fact or a blind destiny, and as a consequence believing that we should take advantage of everything for ourselves alone, crushing everyone else, exploiting every situation. For the loss of the sense of God induces all forms of human degradation. But so long as one has this substantial holy fear of God, he or she, even though a sinner, even though disappointed, frustrated, embittered, and burdened with pessimistic feelings, is held in the hand of the Lord.

The image of the stairway which rests on the earth and whose top reaches heaven shows that God is interested in me, in the events of my life, in the daily difficulties that I alone know, and mysteriously surrounds me and supports me in my endeavors.

2. On this symbol is engrafted the *proclamation*, "And there was the Lord standing beside him and saying: 'I, the Lord, am the God of your forefather Abraham and the God of Isaac' '' (v. 13). The face of God is personally shown to Jacob: *I am*, and the divine presents itself in a friendly, familial way.

Sometimes we find ourselves in an unfamiliar locale, and suddenly someone comes up to us and says: I'm so-and-so, a friend of your parents, I know who you are. In our text from Genesis God is similarly revealed: I am the Lord, the One who made heaven and earth. But I am also the God of your father Abraham, and the God of Isaac. I know you, I know your family and the problems that afflict you all. I know your father, who is all but senile and no longer able to keep a hand on his affairs. I know your mother, who is too weak to reconcile you two brothers. I know the reasons for which you have fled. I know you intimately.

This second revelation is profoundly important because God is revealed as a friend, a friend who knows the human heart and its vacillating emotions. God knows you, is your friend, and understands where you truly are.

3. The *promise*. Referring to Abraham and Isaac, the Lord unreservedly reconfirms the promises that are then expressed in an extraordinary and unexpected way. Gently, God gathers up the meaningful reference points in Jacob's life—the land, his heritage, the covenant, the divine protection during the journey—and makes Jacob understand that all is held in the hand of God.

There is first of all the promise about the *land*: "The land on which you are lying I will give to you and your descendants" (v. 13b). This land in which Jacob felt himself to be lost, on which he was afraid to go to sleep for fear of wild beasts, is given to him.

It is interesting how the Lord is anxious to relate this man with this land. And here we confront the great mystery of Israel and the role it continues to play in history. Israel cannot do without its own land, for it is with the land that God constituted a people. If we do not understand this, we will never understand the political mystery of Israel and the mystery of the Jews.

With the promise of the land comes the promise of *descendants*, of Jacob's relationship with a family he has not yet begun: "These shall be as plentiful as the dust of the earth, and through them you shall spread out east and west, north and south" (v. 14a). Note the disproportion between what Jacob was seeking (saving his life) and the promise of numberless descendants. This causes his reference points to be, so to speak, blown apart. God expands for Jacob the horizon of his relationship with his own kind.

The third promise concerns the *nations*: "In you and your descendants all the nations of the earth shall find blessing" (v. 14b). Jacob had thought, at the most, of himself, his family, and his own immediate people. But the word of God opens him to the whole of humanity, showing us that it is not morally or spiritually possible for one to consider oneself only within the narrow confines of one's family and culture.

Gradually, some 3500–4000 years after Jacob, humanity is understanding the depths of this text. We can think, for example, of what John Paul II in his encyclical *Sollicitudo rei socialis* has called *global interdependence*: that is, the impossibility of any civilized people and nation undergoing fair and just economic and social development without somewhat embracing all other peoples and nations. This is a new horizon that did not exist at the beginning of the century and that presently and insistently imposes itself upon us, demanding that persons responsible for economic and financial growth think in terms of a planetary ethic.

In our biblical passage, God's plan has such vastness: *all the nations of the earth.*

Then the Lord specifies the never-changing center of the *covenant*: "Know that I am with you" (v. 15a). It is the key word of the covenant, this mystery of the indestructible union that God wishes to definitively institute with humankind and that, beginning with Abraham, reaches all human beings in and through Jesus Christ. It is the formula pronounced by the angel to Mary, "The Lord is with you" (Luke 1:28), and that Jesus says at the end of his life, "Know that I am with you always, until the end of the world!" (Matt 28:20).

God reveals himself not only as *the* global, universal point of reference for everyone, as the One who protects the development of all human beings, but as the One who wishes to be the unique reference point, the fundamental, privileged, and indestructible point of reference for each individual person. You will recall that on our earlier retreat together we considered the brief formula from the Song of Songs, "My love belongs to me and I to him" (Cant 6:3), I am yours and you are mine. Jacob already senses this divine intimacy that will express itself in the Eucharist and be fully realized in the Beatific Vision when all humanity will be redeemed in Christ.

The last promise is the *specific protection* that will be given to him on his journey: "I will protect you wherever you go, and bring you back to this land. I will never leave you until I have done what I promised you" (v. 15b).

Jacob's journey, one that seems a venture into the unknown, a leap in the dark, is from first to last presided over by the Lord. It has not been chosen principally by his mother Rebekah, nor even by Jacob himself. In reality all of it has been in the hands of God.

4. It is easy at this point to understand Jacob's exclamation: "When Jacob awoke from his sleep, he exclaimed, 'Truly, the Lord is in this spot, although I did not know it!' " (v. 16). He makes the extraordinary discovery of one who sees himself at the center of God's plans for him and he now reinterprets his whole life in such a way—including his being alone, on journey, a poor fugitive—that he acquires clarity in his mind and encouragement in his spirit.

Such are reflections that we can make comparing Jacob's apparent situation (where he thinks he is) and his true one (where he really is).

Now that Jacob has come to see his actual situation, he is like a new man. He has a mission and a zeal for the journey that now he will confidently face.

### Where I am

We are now invited to an analysis in two phases as we try to apply the biblical narrative to our own experience.

A first phase will consist in meditation on the visible coordinates or reference points of our life; a second phase will be to seek the invisible ones. Only in this embracive context will it in fact be possible to conduct a true discernment of God's word for each one of us. These meditations will be expressed in the first person, but each one of you can apply the principles to your own lives.

1. The *visible coordinates of my life.* First of all I would like to underline the fact that typically we do not know ourselves

very well. Recently, I was reading a report on the pastoral care of young people which sharply set in relief how even a young person who is consciously seeking his or her vocation is typically little known by their spiritual advisors and little known also by themselves:

> The first thing to consider attentively is the young person him/herself, what that person's real life situation is, what the context is in which the person lives, his/her personal and faith history, what the person is seeking and what motivation spurs this search, what degree of docility the young person manifests and what kind of desire or willingness to be counselled. . . . All of this constitutes the object of a delicate and demanding research in which it is important not to move hastily and to try to understand with precision. At times I find that priests and religious who send me a young person for vocational discernment or for spiritual help think they know that person, but in fact they know him or her very little. They know the expressed ideas of the young man or woman but almost nothing of their real habits, of their history, or their family. I have the impression that in recent years we have fallen into a certain disincarnate spiritualism and that paradoxically we undervalue the influences and conditionings of life as these bear upon the choices we make. I say 'paradoxically' because in other ways our culture is saturated with psychological and psychoanalytic concerns. But these psychological evidences are for the most part used by those of us in religious life to guide and adjust our evaluation of objective or subjective moral acts, by what someone *does*. Beyond this there is the deeper question of what one *is*. I repeat: it seems to me that there is a great deal of superficiality in our understanding of persons. Pressured with work, educators unfortunately do not have much time to dedicate to this patient research.

It is precisely this deep personal knowledge that I think each one of us must attain for oneself, and I suggest some fundamental reference points or coordinates on which you can dwell more or less at length, depending on how much material each coordinate would furnish you in your own life.

One tangible reference point concerns *the life of relationships,* above all those with family and with friends.

It is very useful to ask oneself: How am I really situated in my family, what are my real relationships in it? We often neglect and undervalue the positive dynamics in family life. We may also disregard negative or perverse ones that are sometimes created and which—precisely because they are not carefully considered—continue to re-emerge and cause problems. Sometimes after having made certain choices we become aware that these were conditioned by uncritically assumed family attitudes.

It seems to most of us that we instinctively see our own family in a clear light, but every example of parental and sibling relationships, or of relationships in the more extended family, is made up of lights and shadows, both of which condition us a great deal. The Bible tells many stories of the patriarchs which show us healthy, and wounded, relationships with parents and siblings.

Among the many letters I receive, I was much struck by that of a very young girl who, among other things, said to me: "I was very happy with your visit" (an allusion of my coming to her parish) "and I would like to ask you some things. Could you write a letter to my father and tell him to give up drinking between meals so that he won't get drunk? And make him understand that he shouldn't smoke in the kitchen or other rooms but only in the hall. . . . When you write to my father I hope you can add some words to my mother and aunts to deepen their Christian faith." The letter is interesting to me because the young girl sees a difficulty in her family situation and describes it just as it is, expressing at the same time her concern that her family does not live the deep faith that she feels herself to have.

Family relationships exist so profoundly inside us that in one degree or another they condition our choices, consciously or unconsciously; and we ought to recognize and accept this. Sometimes, for example, there are religious vocations in which one is unconsciously influenced by a desire to get away from one's family and some heavy suffering associated with the family. This is not to say that such a religious decision cannot be the will of God—for even through such wounded family situations God is able to elicit an authentic choice—but it is well that these choices be clarified and that one knows the dynamics that operate in one's psyche.

Among our relationships *friendships* ought to be considered, and at the same time their opposites, enmities. We must honestly ask ourselves whether among our close associates we are or are not being understood, being welcomed or rejected, supported or mocked, put on a pedestal or snubbed. The dynamics of these relationships outside the family also play into our great choices according to how, within our circles of associates, we experience various attractions and repulsions.

Another tangible or visible coordinate is what the Bible calls *the land*, and which among other things includes the body, work and study, and money.

Concerning one's body, one has to consider the factors of health, physical development, physical possibilities or impossibilities. No one has perfect health, and we are absolutely limited by *our weaknesses*, by what we would like to do but simply cannot. And then there is the role that depression and low spirits play in our life, and all the variations of our inner dispositions and temperament. There is the part played by sensuality in the widest sense: imagination, the spontaneous arousal of feelings and desires, sexuality—all that pertains in my relationship with my body. Since the body is in fact part of the earth it ought to be managed as a blessing which God has given me, and I ought to question myself about what and how many physical goods I use; this, regarding eating, drinking, smoking, and entertainment—all are ways through which I relate to my body.

*Work*—or for some persons, *study*, which is a form of work—is that toil by which one submits to the demands of the earth. By means of study I ordinarily acquire the ideas that allow me to dominate and subdue the earth. Everyone ought to ask themselves what is the inner life and reason for their study, is it simply something to be endured, does it proceed from excessive curiosity, or is it more integral: an effort to understand and be in positive equilibrium with reality? Apart from the misery of tragic imbalances—such as anti-socialness, the use of drugs, etc.—modest daily struggles exist that exact a toilsome discipline from us. It is important therefore to have an objective, disenchanted, and persevering attitude respecting our work and study.

*Money* is also a factor in our physical life, and about it we may ask: What use do I make of it? Do I tend to greed or, on the contrary, do I take little account of money or use it badly? The kind of attention that I give or do not give to money helps to determine my personality.

Were there time, this discussion would have to be enlarged to include our personal relationship with society, culture, politics, sports, and so on. Each one of you is able to reflect for yourselves on your own experience and see how you are situated with respect to all these realities which constitute what we may call the furniture of our world.

One last coordinate that is suggested to me by the story of Jacob's journey is *the future*. Do I fear the future? Do I anticipate it? How do I see the relationship between my future and the choices to which I am now called? Am I afraid of not making the right choices?

I have simply indicated a series of common visible coordinates in life. As you consider these things I think it would be useful for you to write responses to certain questions, the answers to which significantly describe you. These are the same questions Jacob would have been able to reflect upon before going asleep: Who and how am I? Where am I? What is happening to me?

2. The coordinates that are *invisible* are the most real in our existence. As was said in the tale of *The Little Prince*, invisible

things are seen with the heart and are therefore the things that count most of all.

We can take up again the three coordinates that we have seen expressed in the passage about Jacob: Providence as the general background or condition, the Word, and the Promise.

How am I situated in the face of Providence, that is, *what sense of God do I have in my life?* Perhaps I experience God to be present to me, comforting me; perhaps I know that God cares for and sustains me. Or, I find God is absent, eclipsed by my trials and troubles, by the temptation of atheism, by unbelief, by my various tactics of escape. We have to realize that these trials through which we pass are not only negative realities; they also constitute part of the dynamics of our connections or relationships with the invisible order.

What *sense of the Word do I have?* In particular, how do I stand with respect to the living revelation that is Jesus Christ and with respect to the written revelation that is the Bible, especially the Gospels?

Perhaps in the manner of Jacob I have to admit: Truly, the word of God was all around me, and I did not know it so it counted little in my life.

Or, perhaps I do entrust myself to the Word but often go through trying times of weariness and darkness.

The word of God is a *promise*, a promise also intended for me, and it translates into the formula: I will be with you, I *am* with you. God is not only the God of my father, of my people and ancestry, of my tradition and culture, of my local church, but is the God *for me* and with me.

To make the word of God *as* promise alive and present in us is very fundamental for every life choice, including the most difficult ones. The instinctive fear and anxiety I experience as I face certain choices indicate a lack of the sense of God's promise.

Some of us may have to accept, in some sense even choose, a life of suffering. How many times have I met young people who, through some misfortune, through a progressive and painful illness, are confined to a wheel-chair; and I have had the joy of seeing that God's word as promise (I am with you!) has become a renewal of life for them. The promise of the Lord illuminated their existence in an extraordinary form.

Only in this way can the human being face the sometimes painful and often arduous journey of life and be enabled to choose the difficult actions and vocations that God's word proposes to us.

We can ask Mary, to whom the promise made to Jacob was repeated (the Lord is with you!), to help us hear better, especially today, this word of divine promise in our lives.

I also invite you to seek other pages in Scripture where and how the reassuring affirmation *I will be with you* is expressed.

# Entering into the Mystery
# of the Passover

Homily for Friday of the fifteenth week of the year
Liturgical texts: Exodus 11:10-12, 14; Matthew 12:1-8

During these days together let us allow ourselves to be inspired by the liturgical readings, certain that the words of the Lord, chosen by the Church, can nourish our spirit at this very time when we are making great efforts to determine God's will in our lives.

Two of the texts we have heard proclaimed are fundamental.

## The sign of the Passover

We hear the first text (Exod 11:10-12, 14) read every year during the Easter Vigil. It tells us of the central moment in the history of Israel and foreshadows the supreme event in the whole history of salvation. This particular passage has a cultic, sacrificial element, and implicitly refers to the temple, the center of Jewish worship. But it is not the only description of the Passover that we find in Scripture. Many other passages mentioning and renewing the Passover do so in a variety of Israel's historical settings, showing again and again how this fundamental event in the life of the chosen people had been variously lived, recalled, and handed down.

First of all, we gather from the passage the connection the Passover has with the daily existence of the people and also with the importance of the seasons of the year: ''The Lord said to Moses and Aaron in the land of Egypt, 'This month shall stand at the head of your calendar' '' (Exod 12:1-2). The biblical person feels him/herself to be part of the earth and is aware of their human involvement with physical and cosmic cycles. It is proper therefore to sanctify, with a specific rite, the return of life during the first lunar phase in the spring. The rite, the sacrificing of a lamb, recalls Israel's beginnings in rural experience. The rite is, of course, a symbolic act indicating God's sovereignty over all creation. It also recalls a primordial human experience, the sacrifice offered by Abel, shepherd of flocks.

We can say therefore that the Jews were recalling, in the Passover, their complex human tangible coordinates, that is, their essential connections with the physical world. They acknowledged that their very humanity was characterized by contact with nature, with work, with all the events and elements that are part of our physical existence and that the passage from Exodus represents.

These human coordinates are, nevertheless, subordinate to the divine coordinates. The human being is not only in connection and dialog with nature, with one's own body, with the seasons, with work, with the herds and flocks; at the same time he or she lives all of this in dialog with God. Such an encompassing earthly, human, and divine dialog grasps the human person precisely in the moment in which one becomes aware of one's bond with all of visible and invisible reality. And such a dialog gives one an opening of love, of salvation, of enduring and progressive liberation.

The Passover is the event in which all the agricultural, pastoral, human traditions of Israel are invested with the certainty that God has all things in hand, and remembers the chosen people in order to free them, in order to love them again and again, in order to tell them that the Lord is near and will never forget them.

This fidelity of God characterizes the whole of the Old Testament. In and through the Jews God teaches all of us to understand ourselves in the light of the encompassing global coordinates or connections that form us, without neglecting any of them, in order to live our lives in full harmony, authenticity, and faith.

The sign of the Passover continues today. After thousands of years, we Christians still celebrate it with the fullness and meaning that Jesus gave to it. Today the Christian Passover or paschal mystery still includes bread, wine, the earth, the seasons, human production, economics, the meal, the feast, society, the communion of souls. But all of this is now invested with the mystery of Christ, who reveals the love of a provident God who looks after each one of us and who desires a true and just life for each of us.

The daily Passover that unites our life now is the Eucharist, the vast mystery by which God wishes to bring the human being to the perfection of Christ. The Eucharist touches us intimately, unites us with God and one another, and gives us even a physical certitude that God is with us.

When I eat the Eucharistic bread and drink the blood of Christ, I feel myself to be in contact with that divine mystery that gives unity to my existence and to all of history. It is this mystery which orients me towards the truest horizon and enables me to come to authentic choices of life vocations.

The meaning of the Passover in Christ is not completely expressible in words. Rather, we are invited to enter into the mystery of the liturgy, into silent adoration, into contemplation of the crucifix, into reflection on ourselves.

As Church we celebrate the Passover, but in reality it is the Passover that envelopes us on all sides. It is important to see ourselves inside this mystery, the mystery of the infinite love of the Father, who in the Son rejoins humanity through the grace of the Holy Spirit, enabling human beings to experience even physically the power of God's presence, on the cross, and in the meal that is the Christian Eucharist.

Let us ask the Lord that we might be able to live, during the days of this retreat, all the wealth of the Eucharist. We do not ask so much for wondrous insights as for the certainty that everything—ourselves, our unfolding lives, the whole history of humanity—derives from the Passover and is renewed in the Eucharist.

Let us pray. We give you thanks, O God, for the Passover. We praise you and we thank you because by means of this event you continually reconstitute us, re-make and renew us, again and again give us confidence and hope. May we be able to abandon ourselves to this great mystery just as the Eucharist we now celebrate presents it to us.

### The Lord of the Sabbath

The selection from the Gospel according to Matthew (12:1-8) contains words from the prophet Hosea, ones that we often find coming from the mouth of Jesus: "It is mercy I desire and not sacrifice."

To what can we compare and contrast these words of Jesus that would enable us to see how distinctive is the mystery of the incarnate God?

We can contrast it with a rigid and ideological conception of life, to a narrow conception of a paltry and lifeless existence—all of which can be found even in religious contexts and societies. Indeed, Jesus utters these words in disputation with some of the so-called religious persons of his time. Another example of this narrow-mindedness is recorded in chapter nine, again in Matthew. It is told how Jesus went to dine at the house of this same Matthew and how there were other persons at table who were not considered respectable. "The Pharisees saw this and complained to his disciples, 'What reason can the Teacher have for eating with tax collectors and those who disregard the law?' Overhearing the remark, he said: 'People who are in good health do not need a doctor; sick people do. Go and learn the meaning of the words, ''It is mercy I desire and not sacrifice'' ' '' (Matt 9:11-13). As if to say: Since this saying is central in the Old Testament and you have not understood it, you haven't understood the Bible.

Jesus scolds any who presume to be believers, even practicing believers, but who have not understood the substance of God's message.

In our text, the disciples of Jesus are admonished by the Pharisees because on the Sabbath they were gathering ears of corn to eat them.

> When the Pharisees spied this, they protested: ''See here! Your disciples are doing what is not permitted on the sabbath.'' He replied: ''Have you not read what David did when he and his men were hungry, how he entered God's house and ate the holy bread, a thing forbidden to him and his men or anyone other than priests? Have you not read in the law how the priests on temple duty can break the sabbath rest without incurring guilt? I assure you, there is something greater than the temple here. If you understood the meaning of the text, 'It is mercy I desire and not sacrifice,' you would not have condemned these innocent men'' (Matt 12:2-7).

The problem was not their having taken some ears in a corn-field, since the Mosaic law explicitly allowed such actions. Abuse of property and cheating were forbidden, but the Jews had a very humane conception of sharing the goods of the earth.

The disciples were reproved by the Pharisees because they behaved this way on the Sabbath. Perhaps, in the place of Jesus, you and I would have used a more diplomatic or ''politic'' approach with the Pharisees, saying something like this: ''It's true, it is the Sabbath. But it is not strictly forbidden to take the ears of corn. You're right, it's a serious business, but try to excuse them since it's a case of necessity.'' Now, instead, Jesus attacks the Pharisees' objection directly, meeting it head on: You just have not understood the Scriptures. You think you've understood them, but your mentality is ideological, rigid, monolithic, far from the mind of God.

Jesus reveals to us that God is tender, near to human beings and wanting their good. God is not as interested in the regularity of sacrificial offerings—even though these may be necessary—as in everything that fosters true human good. This is the key to Jesus' piety or religiousness, a religiousness that reveals God as One who, before anything else, has humankind's well-being at heart. Everything which restricts and constricts, suffocates the human being, even if under religious or liturgical appearances, is not pleasing to God.

Naturally, the application of the principle that God wills our freedom is not easy, and we ought to fight against any interpretation that is an abuse or misuse of freedom, just as we should struggle against any squelching of divinely given and willed human freedom.

In the light of this Gospel passage, I am confident in assuring you that God wants your full realization, your truest good. God's love is most perfectly exemplified in Jesus, Son of Man, Lord of the Sabbath. In Jesus, God shows what the divine love intends to do for us. And this includes the important, more, the fundamental element of the Cross in our lives. The Father did not spare the Son; rather, it is through the Cross that Jesus attained his fullness.

God desires your fulfillment, the realization of which, however, will not coincide with doing only what is easy and comfortable—for you will have to move beyond meager and half-hearted behavior. And this fulfillment is to follow Jesus, to be like him, to be, in your way, Lord of the Sabbath, Son of Man, greater than the temple.

*Lord, you are greater than the temple, and you are here in the midst of us in the mystery of your Passover. Help us to know you and adore you, Lord, to set before you our fears, pettiness, and rigidity. Enable us to be enlightened by the vastness of your mind and the fullness of your heart, for we know human nature and its need of you. We also know the men and women we are and should be, called to be like you, called to foster authentically the lives of all our brothers and sisters in the human family, even as you have done. Grant, O Lord, that we may find the way to respond to this revelation of God that is given us in the Passover. In the life of Jesus the Passover is day by day made concrete for us, so that we can live it deeply and become more fully ourselves. You, O Father, have from eternity with untiring love willed us to be ourselves. May we be so in Jesus Christ, who with you, in the grace and power of the Holy Spirit, reign for all ages to come.*

# Our Life Coordinates: Lost and Confused

In order to know God's will for us, in order to listen to God's word for our life, we have to purify ourselves of sin.

One of you asked me: why does sin prevent us from knowing our vocation? In order to meet this question it seems to me it would be useful to reflect on what I would like to call, going back to the terms of our previous meditation, *lost or confused coordinates*. The presence of the visible or invisible coordinates, or reference points, allows Jacob to know where he is and to understand what God is saying to him. But what happens when such coordinates are lost or confused?

To answer this, some reflections on sin are needed—on our own personal sin and on what we can call the sin of humanity. In the first part of the meditation I will briefly recall some biblical typologies of sin that are found in the Book of Genesis and that foreshadow the episode about Jacob. These will help to orient us as we try to understand our own wounded situation today.

In the second part I will dwell on some contemporary typologies of sin and weakness but also of goodness.

**Biblical typologies of sin**

In the first chapters of Genesis, the Bible presents us with the three great coordinates which when they are harmoniously fused constitute an ideal for humanity, the fullness of human life. These are the proper relationship with God, other human beings, and the earth. Of course, the Bible shows us that very soon such an ideal was in various ways disregarded and perverted, provoking thereby both the anger and the mercy of God. Everything from then on will converge on the Cross of Christ, the culmination of God's love and the supreme triumph over the confusion and loss of these relationships which continue to characterize humanity.

1. *The story of Cain and Abel*

> In the course of time Cain brought an offering to the Lord God from the fruit of the soil, while Abel, for his part, brought one of the best firstlings of his flock. The Lord looked with favor on Abel and his offering, but on Cain and his offering he did not. Cain greatly resented this and was crestfallen. So the Lord said to Cain: ''Why are you so resentful and crestfallen? If you do well, you can hold up your head; if you do not, sin is a demon lurking at the door: his urge is towards you, yet you can be his master'' (Gen 4:3-7).

Which is the coordinate lost by Cain?

Probably his first mistake was an imperfect or miserly offering. Nevertheless, his sin takes on force and violence in him when he becomes sad and does not accept the fact that his brother is better than he and refuses to live in peace with someone who has a destiny different from his own. Cain does not realize that humanity is constituted by unity in diversity. And rather than feeling himself stimulated to climb up to Abel's stature, he would like his brother to descend to his level. He is living within the sadness of envy, one of the gravest causes of the wars, social conflicts, and various forms of racism that devastate humanity. These dramatic forms of racism are present in our midst, and they will grow in violence in Europe just as the number of persons of other races and cultures increases among us. It will take a great effort from us to live fraternally with blacks, Arabs, and Asiatics. We will have to work very hard to fully accept and live with these peoples, to change our ways, to rejoice in the well-being of others who are different from us.

With downcast heart and profound grievance Cain no longer heard or heeded the voice of God. He had lost the coordinate of spiritual union with his brother and opened himself to murder. When the Lord does forcefully address him, Cain makes light of the situation: "Then the Lord asked Cain, 'Where is your brother Abel?' He answered, 'I do not know. Am I my brother's keeper?' " (v. 9).

2. The second typology, a mysterious one, is in the story of *the sons of God and the daughters of men.*

> When men began to multiply on earth and daughters were born to them, the sons of heaven saw how beautiful the daughters of men were and so they took for their wives as many of them as they chose. Then the Lord said, "My spirit shall not remain in man forever, since he is but flesh. His days shall comprise one hundred and twenty years." At that time the Nephilim appeared on earth (as well as later), after the sons of heaven had intercourse with the daughters of man, who bore them sons. They were the heroes of old, the men of renown" (Gen 6:1-4).

The passage evokes ancient legends and sagas whose real meaning is difficult to determine. The sacred writer nonetheless retains these immemorial fragments in order to offer us a picture of the forgetfulness, loss, and confusion of fundamental life coordinates.

The first coordinate lost is again that of friendship, here the specific friendship of man and woman: "they took for their wives as many of them as they chose." We read here the beginnings of looking upon the woman as an object, as a thing, not as a person or 'thou' with whom a unique and unbreakable exchange occurs. Woman is seen as a form of possession, not in her dignity equal to that of man.

There is another aspect to be noted here, one which we feel vividly today. It is present in the rather obscure mention of the Nephilim, or 'the giants,' as given in some translations. It's almost as though humanity is deceived, and deceives itself, by creating human beings with superhuman, divine powers.

In a similar way we can think, for example, of the current tremendous temptation of biotechnology: taking life in hand, multiplying it, creating new forms of life and new races of human beings. One conjures up a time when the earth would be an object of complete exploitation, and human beings would have to live in human-made satellites. One can conceive of other projects that science, believing itself all-powerful, might elaborate if it no longer restrains itself and loses the delicate balance of humanity with the earth.

The loss of these proper relationships—humanity and the earth, the human person and the body—are tragic. It is imperative that we attend to the natural rhythms of existence which, though they are certainly in continuous evolution and over the which we ought to develop a benign and democratic mastery, cannot be disregarded with impunity.

### 3. *The story of the tower of Babel*

The whole world spoke the same language, using the same words. While men were migrating in the east, they came upon a valley in the land of Shinar and settled there. They said to one another, "Come, let us mold bricks and harden them with fire." They used bricks for stone, and bitumen for mortar. Then they said, "Come, let us build ourselves a city and a tower with its top in the sky, and so make a name for ourselves; otherwise, we shall be scattered all over the earth." The Lord came down to see the city and the tower that the men had built. Then the Lord said: "If now, while they are one people, all speaking the same language, they have started to do this, nothing will later stop them from doing whatever they presume to do. Let us then go down and there confuse their language, so that one will not understand what another says." Thus the Lord scattered them from there all over the earth, and they stopped building the city. That is why it was called Babel, because there the Lord confused the speech of all the world. It was from that place that he scattered them all over the earth (Gen 11:1-9).

What happened? Simply, the invention of bricks. Previously, buildings had been constructed out of wood, or by laying one stone upon another. Thus, houses were only one story high. But bricks were of a relatively light and very manageable form, and with their invention human beings began to think there were no practical limits to human appetites. Humanity would be able to reach heaven through its own efforts.

In itself we are dealing, in the invention of bricks, with a technical fact which is neither good nor bad. Nevertheless, behind the fact we read in the biblical account of the enthusiasm, the presumption, the ambition that can come with discoveries or inventions—a little like the invention today of the computer, of an artificial intelligence we can use to control the world.

"Come, let us build ourselves a city and a tower with its top in the sky, and so make a name for ourselves; otherwise we shall be scattered all over the earth" (v.4). Here we have a great example of sinful pride generated by grandiose projects. Sometimes we think *we* are the ones that give ourselves glory and *we* are the judges of our destiny present and to come, and forever. Then, subtly, without explicit blasphemy, the contact with God is broken. For in truth it is God who makes us great—who "makes a name for us"—God who throws out a bridge or ladder towards us (Jacob's vision is the opposite of the tower of Babel).

Sin does not consist in wanting to construct a tower, but in rupturing the coordinate of the holy fear of God, in forgetting humanity's proper subjection to the Lord of heaven and earth. We are today fully implicated with this temptation, much more than in past centuries because our constant inventions cause us to think we can do anything, that we no longer depend on anything above us, that we give ourselves our very identity or essence. The more we assume vast and powerful social-political and scientific responsibilities the more we are immersed in a mentality in which the essential life coordinates have been lost or confused. Sometimes we are forced to live in a condition of over-excitement and sometimes in a state of depression, discouragement, and bitterness. The temptation to have absolute control of life easily passes over into a sense of complete physical, moral, and spiritual emptiness and a loss of trust in life. And at that point one no longer understands anything.

The biblical typologies that I have briefly recalled deal rather much with our great idolatries and illusions. They show us how we risk being stripped of our coordinates and caught up in a psychological whirlwind in which it is difficult to orient oneself. It is difficult indeed if in our hearts there is no clear sense of the mystery of God and Christ, from which comes a consistent relationship not only with the Lord but also with family, society, work, and economic goods.

## Contemporary typologies

We shall now consider some typologies strongly evident in our contemporary period. I will describe for you several groups of young people who are more or less confused, or clear, about their life coordinates.

1. *The alienated young person.* This is the young man or woman who is not only far from the Church but who has also made some seriously mistaken, destructive choices. Generally, these young people avoid ordinary life in our society. I have encountered them in prisons.

I begin with this category because it is not so hard to imagine ourselves becoming alienated like these unfortunate young people. Recently, a customs official who worked for awhile in southern Italy told me about the thousands of unemployed youth in the south who are first recruited to handle contraband tobacco from Albania and then, getting used to having a lot of money in their pockets, become steady workers in this kind of traffic. These young people are not evil. They can be observed daily, harmlessly chatting in the squares with other young men and women. But little by little they are attracted to the life of this "easy money," and they find themselves in a descending spiral of destructive behavior from which there is no escape.

In other instances, alienated young people are carrying heavy family trials, wounds, "baggage." We ought to pray a great deal for them. They *are* able to change, even to undergo formidable transformations. I think, for example, of the testimony of that young boy whom we all heard at an earlier gathering who had committed murder and yet who has, in prison, once more found the path of faith and spirituality.

I also point out this category of alienated young persons, first, because sometimes we meet these people and we are seized with two opposing temptations, both of them mistaken: the first, an instinctive reaction, is to pigeonhole and prejudge them without appeal; the second is to flatter them, to become a little like them, almost disguising our real selves. Instead of these reactions, we ought to ask of God:

"Lord, help us in these encounters to be truly ourselves, not to be ashamed, not to pretend. Help us not to judge but simply to realize that these young men and women need others to speak the truth to them with love."

The Bible teaches us that God is afraid of no sin. *We* are afraid of certain sins knowing that if we were to commit them or if someone were to commit them against us we would be incapable of forgiving either ourselves or the other person. But ours is a God who never withdraws from us, whose love is always stronger than our sin. And contemplating Jesus on the Cross we know that he was not afraid of taking on himself the sins of the world, including our own sins. For this reason the ministry in prisons, for example, is one of the most beautiful ministries. It puts us in contact with the infinite mercy and love of God which hastens to throw itself into the dark seas of our human sin in order to save us.

2. *The apparently far young person.* This is the category of those who for different reasons—having to do with family, or cultural background, or various prejudices—almost never go to church.

Yet, these people are honest and decent; they have a sense of values. There are many like this, and so one often comes across them. The task is to help them find that real but, to them, unknown relationship expressed in the story of Jacob's dream. That is, we need to help these young persons to recognize God and be able to say: The Lord is here and I did not know it! No doubt the Lord is working in them, but because of the problems and weaknesses in the history of the Church and the defects that sometimes occur in its preaching and teaching, they confuse God with some facsimile of God that is unacceptable. From within the apparently distant young person there may rise one day a definitive religious or other vocation when that person comes to understand the power of the Spirit writing in his, in her heart, even if they do not yet understand it clearly.

3. *The apparently near young person* is a more familiar figure to us here. These people are near because they are to be found in church. Perhaps they work for the Church and are involved in its activities; sometimes they even pledge themselves to the Church.

Yet they are also far, because they give evidence that they have never truly met the Lord. For these persons Christianity is merely an association and a set of customs. Religion is moralistic for them rather than a life of profound human and divine love. Usually, these young people are rather rigid, harsh, and melancholic. They may be critical of the Church and very judgmental of its pastors. They demand a great deal from other persons but one gathers from their lack of mercy that they are not profoundly Christian. For them Christianity is an institution and not the person of Jesus.

This third category is rather widespread, and its members do not have much openness to any Christian vocation since they think they already know the Lord and the Lord's will. What comes to mind are the bitter words of Jesus in John's Gospel: "If you were blind there would be no sin in that. 'But we see,' you say, and your sin remains" (John 9:41).

These apparently near young persons take pleasure in their own kind of thinking and living, and they judge themselves to be responding to God's will, which they think they know. They sometimes judge themselves to be lazy and negligent or moralistically guilty; and they believe that God judges minor infractions heavily. In reality they are far from having understood the Jesus of the Gospels, the Jesus who reveals the Father's love.

Perhaps the greatest suffering in the Church has to do with persons who think they know everything, including all exact inferences in the Church's wisdom; whereas in fact they still have not truly made the decisive step of knowing God. Though it is possible for a religious vocation to develop within these "near" but really distant young people, it will likely take a very rigid form. And if so, those from this group who become priests or religious will not be able to bear up with the trials in ministering the Church's life, for that ministry requires, before everything else, a personal relationship with Jesus and participation in his mercy.

I fear that the intransigent anti-renewal movement of Archbishop Lefebvre and his followers goes, at least in part, along these lines of an institutional rigidity which is unaccompanied by a deep comprehension of the Lord of the Gospels.

4. *The truly near* young person is the one who has had authentic experiences of faith and grace. Not without weaknesses or sins, this person has nonetheless encountered Jesus crucified, known the God of grace and love.

What defects belong to this typology?

The principal defect is somewhat of a constitutional one: an immaturity, inconstancy, and impatience, longing to have everything at once. The truly near young person is surprised, for example, that having prayed a lot he or she has not received consolation and comfort from God, that having been good the experience of joy has not immediately followed.

It is still not clear to these people that God is infinite mercy. They have indeed known the person of Jesus but perhaps have restricted or severely structured their relationship with Jesus, another sign of a still immature faith. These folks are easily deluded about themselves. They consider their own sins as, above all, failures to live up to their own ideal of life; and they are depressed about themselves as Cain was, having downcast faces. They don't look upon their sins as showing a lack of trust in the love of God, as failures of which one repents with love with an open heart. This defect of self-absorption is hard to overcome, and years of constancy and patience are needed to attain a true knowledge of Jesus.

Among these truly near persons some have authentic vocations. These people need a good deal of support in this matter, though, because they are subject to ups and downs. Since persons in this group are easily enough irritated and angry with themselves, they are inclined to conclude that they are not cut out for a religious vocation. Instead, they need to be taught to see their mood swings, their ups and downs as part of Jacob's journey towards his goal.

This fourth type is really very lovely, but it has to be accompanied by daily, persevering prayer.

5. *The mature Christian* is the young person who, having encountered the Lord a number of times in life, having recognized his/her own sin, has entered to such an extent into the mercy of Jesus as to be able to serve God wherever possible and with all one's strength.

Persons in this ideal group are certainly available for any Christian vocation, for having understood the priority of serv-

ice to God and the Gospel, they can tranquilly choose to consecrate themselves in the priesthood, religious life or marriage.
They have indeed clarified the fundamental dimension of
existence.

There is, however, a trial that they have to overcome on
their journey: God is mystery; is light and yet at times is
shrouded in darkness and appears incoherent; comes and goes;
in one moment causes us to perceive the divine presence and
then as suddenly seems to abandon us; causes us to seek and
not to find in order that we seek the divine life all the more.
Our maturity grows in the patient and persevering search of
a God who never lets us rest on our laurels but asks us to continuously set ourselves back on the road and move deeper into
life and the divine reality.

6. The last category is a subordinate part of the preceding
one and it is that of *young persons who look beyond.*

These are Christians solid in the faith yet having perhaps
some personality limitations and not being as wise and well-
rounded as the mature Christian. They desire a very great
adhesion to Jesus, to his life and to his death. It is not so much
the drive to serve the Gospel that characterizes them as the
urge to be always more like Jesus.

There is in these persons a thirst for the radical that the mature Christian does not always have, and such a thirst reveals
itself in the fact that these people vibrate easily with the most
misunderstood and least popular aspects of Christianity: the
Cross, silence, absolute poverty, the seclusion of the cloister,
the pardon of enemies, the Beatitudes, undergoing insults and
humiliations for the love of Jesus.

This is a very interesting typology and it is also to be found
among the youth whom we described as ''truly near.''

What danger does this sort of person have to deal with?
Of course, not the danger of loving Jesus too much, for even
a sufficiently great love of Jesus does not exist, since the mystery of God infinitely superabounds our capacity of love. The

danger lies rather in an irrational radicalism, one that wants to express itself in forms that go against the Gospel itself. It is therefore absolutely necessary that this young person who looks beyond lives a strict relationship with the Church, the Christian community and the parish, has benefit of a spiritual guide, and devotedly attends to the teaching of the magisterium. These people ought not to let themselves go along with immediate and superficial impulses, but persevere in humility and hiddenness.

Let us think of St. Francis of Assisi, who is an example of this type. Being himself well-directed by the Church of his time, he produced much fruit. Others, instead, not having lived in relationship and reference to the Church, ended up in heretical or abnormal forms. As I said, the risk does not come from radicalism in itself—an ever greater love for Jesus is extremely precious—but in expressing it in actions and ways of living not well fitting in the Christian community.

A second danger with this group is that these young people are apt to advert to their personal, psychological, cultural limits and be seized with the fear of not being equal to life and their great burning desires. If the fear is greater than their radicalism, they end by clipping their wings, by closing down the horizons of their life, by inhibiting their hearing of the Word. The error here is an excessive distrust of oneself, the fear of not being up to the demands of the Christian calling, of falling into the net of Satan, who suggests: It's impossible that God has chosen you; you don't deserve it.

What is therefore needed for these young people is a great confidence in the Lord, who does not focus on our merits, who is inside us as a consuming fire, and who calls us constantly to a love of God beyond all measure.

## Conclusion

The typologies that I have exposed for you suggest the immense variety of the humanity in which we are immersed. I must add, though, that these categories are never rigid and foursquare. For example, all of us are to some slight extent implicated in the "alienated" group insofar as we are sometimes subject to temptations of rebellion and escape. In any case, the description I have offered you will be useful for knowing yourselves and also for preparing yourselves for a good confession.

I always counsel in such retreats as this to make a confession comprising three basic dimensions: the confession of praise, the confession of life, and the confession of faith.

The confession of praise consists in asking oneself: For what do I feel grateful to the Lord? What gifts has God given me and continues to give me? Such an examination helps to put ourselves confidently before God—the God who is love, mercy, goodness and kindness itself for us.

After having recognized the love of the Lord, we make the confession of life, which consists in asking oneself: What above all do I dislike in myself? What would I like not to be the case with me? Perhaps what we dislike most are not our sins properly speaking but various deficient and ignoble attitudes and feelings, and strained or melancholic moods—little things that close up the heart. We confess them, desiring thereby to throw ourselves open more fully to the will of God.

Finally, in the confession of faith, we proclaim: I believe, Lord, that are you are merciful and that you save me from my dullness and confusion, from my sin and discord, from my illusions, sadnesses, depressions, and discouragements. I believe that you alone save me and you alone purify me.

In such a way we express before God what we truly are, and we can then ask for the grace of the confession:

*Lord, you who in baptism and confirmation came to me with your Spirit, deepen within me today the power of the Holy Spirit and reconstitute a harmony in me, in faith, in joy, in the peace of your love.*

# Visible Signs
# of the Invisible Coordinates

We want now to reflect on the aftermath and implications of Jacob's dream in order to see how he fixes his experience of God in his mind and memory and in what other ways he responds to the encounter with God.

Jacob has opened his eyes; he has grasped the invisible connections or coordinates of his life. These invisible coordinates clarify the visible ones and give order, joy, confidence, energy, perspective and mission to his existence.

### The signs placed by Jacob

When Jacob awoke from his sleep, he exclaimed, "Truly, the Lord is in this spot, although I did not know it!" In solemn wonder he cried out: "How awesome is this shrine! This is nothing else but an abode of God, and that is the gateway to heaven!" Early the next morning Jacob took the stone that he had put under his head, set it up as a memorial stone, and poured oil on top of it. He called that site Bethel, whereas the former name of the town had been Luz. Jacob then made this vow: "If God remains with me, to protect me on this journey I am making and to give me enough bread to eat and clothing to wear, and I come back safe to my father's house, the Lord shall be my God. This stone that I have set up as a memorial stone shall be God's abode. Of everything you give, I will faithfully return a tenth part to you" (Gen 28:16-22).

Jacob could simply have enjoyed the experience of that night, and afterwards said: It has been wonderful, I thank the Lord, and now I take up my journey again with joy and confidence. But he takes the dream more seriously than that and feels himself obliged to do something in the light of the gift. Appropriately, he expresses some visible signs of the invisible coordinates, of his experience of God.

First, we read in his initial exclamation ("Truly, the Lord is in this spot, although I did not know it!") an expression of his wonder, his gratitude.

Immediately after, however, we read: "In solemn wonder he cried out: 'How awesome is this shrine! This is nothing else but an abode of God, and that is the gateway to heaven!' " This statement elicits and expresses his sense of responsibility. What has happened to him is a privilege, a fact that he was unable to anticipate, that has placed him in a particular relationship with the living God, a relationship from which he is no longer able to withdraw.

Jacob understands that no one is the same after seeing the Lord, and he needs to respond to his blessed experience. This consciousness of his responsibility does not remain a vague sentiment but he concretizes his joy and obligation with some visible signs.

1. "Early the next morning," at the hour of prayer and adoration, "Jacob took the stone that he had put under his head, set it up as a memorial stone." It is a very simple gesture, evidence of the poor circumstances of his life, but a gesture that has great meaning. He wishes to erect this *stone*, one like any other before his action, as a *sign* to indicate that he does not intend to forget what has happened; he wishes to set this stone up as a testimony of the relationship between himself and God. A stone, that ordinarily is simply lying upon the ground, is prominently placed in order to underline that the event and the spot is of a moral and spiritual, and not merely a natural and geological, character.

We know that this simple kind of memorial is one of the earliest religious expressions of humankind. If you go to certain prehistoric sites, in Sardinia, for example, you will find rocks erected as a sign of veneration in memory of some event of long ago. Such rudimentary signs are also part of pagan religions, used to record significant religious happenings.

As further examples of this, let us read from at least two other biblical episodes.

First of all, there is the passage in which Moses embodies the pact with God: "Moses then wrote down all the words of the Lord and, rising early the next day, he erected at the foot of the mountain an altar and twelve pillars for the twelve tribes of Israel" (Exod 24:4). The sign is the same as the one Jacob used even though Moses set up twelve stones, since this later covenant is made not with a single human being or a single family, but with an entire people. Nevertheless, the sign expresses the intention to memorialize an important event through a simple physical act.

A second passage: "So Joshua made a covenant with the people that day and made statutes and ordinances for them at Shechem, which he recorded in the book of the law of God. Then he took a large stone and set it up there under the oak tree that was in the sanctuary of the Lord. And Joshua said to all the people, 'This stone shall be our witness, for it has heard all the words which the Lord spoke to us. It shall be a witness against you, should you wish to deny your God' " (Josh 24:25-27).

In such instances the rocks have been set up as a sign that God has spoken and that we have heard the Lord. It is as though we said: A responsibility has been given to us and this shows we have taken it into account.

2. A second sign is the *oil*: "Jacob took the stone, set it up as a memorial stone, and poured oil on top of it."

Here we have another ancient action, coming down to us in baptismal, confirmational, and priestly consecration. It expresses God's Spirit taking hold of the person. It expresses the sacredness of the person, his belonging to the Lord.

Even if there is no necessary physical reason for using the oil, it serves to symbolize the meaning of the sacred action: as the oil penetrates wherever it is poured or placed upon the body, so the Spirit of God penetrates into the anointed person and remains there.

Finally, Jacob makes *a vow* in the hope of bringing out the meaning and reality of his memorial act as much as possible. He wants to remind himself intensively of God's gift to him that night even as he vows to repay God when the promise of the Lord is fulfilled.

### Present, on-going, and living memorials

What does this ancient piety have to say to us, a piety that tries to express itself with the simple materials and gestures it has at its disposal?

1. *In general* it says that it is dangerous to leave our gifted intuitions vaguely in the mind and memory. Often in our life there are moments of grace, of a true awareness of God. But they begin to erode, to grow less, are forgotten, not because they were unimportant, but rather because we have not taken the trouble to somehow fix them in our memory.

The law of the memorial—and Christianity is founded on that memorial of the death of the Lord called the Eucharist—is a biological, psychological, and spiritual law. It should not be neglected. Otherwise, enthusiasm vanishes, the original spiritual impulse or desire fades, the wonderful ideas we had are dissolved.

In effect, Jacob cautions us to establish visible signs of the decisive invisible coordinates in our life.

2. The biblical narrative suggests that we express *some particular*, visible sign of the invisible coordinates. Then attention to this sign will comfort and reassure us in our recurring emotional slumps.

Let us consider here the chief particular memorials to be found in the Church. I will call them the memorial of Presence; the plural, unfolding, and historical memorial of Scripture; and the living memorial of the inner anointing by the Spirit of God.

The memorial of fullness and presence is the *Eucharist*, present in the sacrifice of the Mass, in Communion, and in the form of the Real Presence in the monstrance and tabernacle. Great is the privilege of living in a parish, a city, anywhere in which the Eucharist, this revelation of the infinite love of God, is a daily presence. I remember being one evening in Tel Aviv, by the sea, in a hotel where we had been brought by the airline company. Looking out from the terrace at the city I said to myself: How sad, there is no Eucharistic presence here.

And I felt myself to be suffocating as I was aware of the difference with our cities full of churches and belltowers.

It is therefore an immense grace to be able to enter into a church to visit the Blessed Sacrament; and not everyone has this privilege. Let us try to deepen—perhaps with the aid of some reading on the meaning of the liturgy and the sacraments—our sense of the value of the Eucharist, this divine food that nourishes our life and without which we would be nothing. From the memoirs of priests who were prisoners in jails or concentration camps it appears their main anxiety was not being able to celebrate the Eucharist—or at least of establishing a time in the day for saying the Mass even if they were unable to consecrate—because they had such need of this formidable point of reference.

The unfolding memorial is the *Bible*. While the Eucharist is like a summation of God's gifts, Scripture is the continuous spelling out and articulation of these gifts. To read the Bible is to bring to mind the invisible reference points of our life. And I do not know a better way, after daily Mass, for making God's gifts present and active in us than a meditative, prayerful reading of the Sacred Texts. I think one of the greatest graces of my life was having learned, when I was ten or eleven years old, the habit of reading the Bible daily. This practice has given me so very much, and without it I would not be able to humanly, spiritually progress. When for reasons of emergency or the press of duties I happen to set aside Scripture meditation, it takes an enormous exertion for me to find myself again, to restore the clarity of my life bearings or coordinates.

Scripture therefore is a continuously present memorial that is able to be with me wherever I am. To develop the habit of reading it in a somewhat systematic way, and praying it, constitutes a formidable instrument for knowing the will of God for you.

Learn how to find yourself more and more deeply in your leisurely reading of the Bible, knowing that God is revealed to you through the constant nourishment of the sacred words.

Perhaps starting out with the Gospels and the Acts of the Apostles, you might then read the letters of St. Paul and after that Exodus, Genesis, and the prophet Isaiah. Scripture is not a flat tableland or plain, where everything is on the same level. It is, rather, a rich panorama of mountains, hills, and lakes; and one has eventually to grasp all of this in its unity. But that happens only in a patient trek through Scripture, and by availing yourself along the way of the marginal notations inviting you to look at various related pages in the Bible.

So, the Bible is a very important memorial which if we are really present to it and it lives in us, will increase our knowledge of the divine coordinates in our life. By reading and rereading Scripture, we will derive a great joy from discovering each day new things to fill us with light and peace.

The Bible and the Eucharist are a little like the stone erected by Jacob, an on-going and fully present memorial of God's gift.

The New Testament reveals what is our truest, most sublime experience of *anointing*: it is God's own self in our heart, it is the Holy Spirit praying in us as a living memorial.

We need to learn how to pray not principally through our own power but by consenting to the prayer that the Spirit of God utters in us.

The basic text to consider, one that we can never meditate on enough, is from St. Paul's Letter to the Romans: "The Spirit too helps us in our weakness, for we do not know how to pray as we ought"—none of us knows how to pray suitably, and this is not surprising—"but the Spirit himself makes intercession for us with groanings that cannot be expressed in speech. He who searches hearts knows what the Spirit means, for the Spirit intercedes for the saints as God himself wills" (Rom 8:26-27). The Holy Spirit asks in us and for us in order that we might know the designs and will of God in our life.

For this reason our prayer is to be an evermore conscious abandonment to the motion of the Spirit in us.

This motion is both ascending and descending. We have to keep on trying to cultivate the ascending movement. It is the activity of praise, even when we are tired and dry, so that we say: I praise you, my God. I thank you because you are great, because you are greater than I, because you perform marvels I do not understand. I bless you and I exalt you above everything and all things, O my God.

This is already prayer in the Spirit and it is very invigorating for our souls.

The descending movement is the request for grace, for mercy and pardon. Among the descending prayers, and having a special place as a memorial, is the sacrament of penance. In this sacrament the Spirit purifies me and prays in me. That prayer of God's Spirit becomes an efficacious action of the Church. And my prayer, asking to be purified of that which I do not know how to conquer and overcome, is entrusted to the Church. Into my prayer as I partake of the sacrament enters the grace of the Holy Spirit, who descends on me in order to encourage me, in order to put me again at peace with myself and my world, in order to reconcile me with my lot and my limits, with my destiny.

This is the anointing or ointment of the Spirit that continually re-invigorates and renews in us the gifts of understanding and wisdom that God has given us.

But since the effects of the Eucharist, Scripture, and the anointing of the Spirit have not only to remain but grow in us, we should note the important matter of *a written statement*.

Perhaps Jacob did not know how to write, and so in that night when he found himself destitute of practically everything, he expressed himself in spoken words while looking upon the symbolic stone. The written word, however, appears very early in the symbolic actions of Israel. Moses "wrote down all the words of the Lord" (Exod 24:4), and Joshua "recorded [these things] in the book of the law of God" (Josh 24:26). The memorial thus becomes a written record. Concerning the salvific deeds of the past, the Bible is this record; concerning my own reality, the written statement is what we can call *the rule of life*.

It is very helpful for us to translate this system of visible signs, of which I have indicated some fundamental coordinates, into a more articulated rule of life that should then be shared with a spiritual guide. What sort of thing ought this rule of life include even if, obviously, there is no one particular, required structure for everyone?

The rule of life ought to set forth some general principles, some thoughts that have significantly touched me and motivate my life. Then, after these general principles, I should write down some precise memorial in the form of spiritual resolutions and self-understanding: when and how I intend to pray every day, how to pray every week, what are the spiritually dangerous and destructive occasions for me and what are ones that foster my life in God.

The writing of a rule of life is a completely free act. But if it is done, it will be an important act, for it guards us from our constant tendency to allow the life of faith to sag, to forget who and where we truly are, and to re-enter into the banality and confusion of daily secularized existence.

Let us prayerfully ask for the intercession of Jacob that we, too, may establish—in a society that does not know the fundamental coordinates—the tangible and visible expressions of the interior life of grace.

# The True Search for God

Homily commemorating Mary Magdalen
Liturgical texts: Canticle of Canticles 3:1-4; John 20:11-18

The celebration of the memory of Mary Magdalen, together with the readings that the liturgy proposes to us as fitting, cause us to reflect on that archetype of the human spirit expressed by the famous psychologist Carl Jung as the *animus* and the *anima*, a twofold principle that exists in a more or less united way in every human being.

The *animus* is the rational, domineering, logical, constructing, and calculating principle, while the *anima* is the receptive and tender principle, the capacity to know others intuitively and "from the heart." All this may also be expressed in a certain respect by the masculine and feminine principles, taking into account, however, that it is the ensemble of the two principles that comprise the archetype of the complete, whole person, whether male or female.

The figure of Mary Magdalen, as it is presented to us in Scripture, is the archetype of the *anima*, of that human quality in the individual person and society which is manifested by intuition, by generous receptivity, by tenderness, by the capacity to understand persons in depth. The liturgy largely limits itself to contemplating, in this saint, this factor that constitutes the most hidden and difficult-to-define aspect of the human spirit, an aspect that if neglected produces a dictatorial, willful and rigid, almost inhuman personality.

It would be interesting to comment on the two readings for today, trying to grasp the relationship between *animus* and *anima* in the completeness of the human psyche and to see how the religious consciousness views the two of them. On the one hand, we have the reasonableness of faith, theology as an intellectual discipline, the perception of the values of visible things and activities. On the other hand, there are the complementary features of mysticism, adoration, ecstasy, praise, profound and unspeakable joy, the tenderness of faith, contemplation of the crucifix. We are always leaning a little in one way or the other, and we need to reflect and act on both in order to join them into a unity in which all the coordinates of the person are grounded.

Not having time to dwell on both readings, I will limit myself to underlining a meaning in the passage taken from the Canticle of Canticles.

### "I sought him but I did not find him"

"On my bed at night I sought him whom my heart loves—I sought him but I did not find him. I will rise then and go about the city; in the streets and crossings I will seek him whom my heart loves. I sought him but I did not find him. The watchmen came upon me as they made their rounds of the city: Have you seen him whom my heart loves? I had hardly left them when I found him whom my heart loves" (Cant 3:1-4).

What strikes me first of all is the repeated line: "I sought him but I did not find him." How would the *animus* interpret this sentence, recalling that it is the calculating, efficient aspect of us? It would say something like this: If you haven't found him, that means that he is not for you, that perhaps he is too far above you, that you are not made for him, that you are on the wrong path.

Instead, the *anima*, working at a deeper level, intuits a different meaning.

I recall the title of a book written by an atheist, in which our words from the Canticle of Canticles were given in Latin: *"Quaesivi et inveni"* (I sought but I did not find). In the book the author recounted his search for God, saying he had not rationally succeeded in finding God. This person was evidently restricted to the *animus* level of the soul, and having sought God through rational proofs alone at a certain point he grew tired of the search. But the complete personality is the one who says: I sought him and since I did not find him I continue to seek him with a still greater love.

I did not find him near to me, so: "I will rise then and go about the city; in the streets and crossings I will seek him whom my heart loves." Here we catch a glimpse of an inner ecstasy and the hidden presence of God, who is working in the center of our souls.

This is important in order to understand ourselves in depth. There exists in all of us a dynamic longing for God, a longing that becomes even more vibrant when we have not found the One whom we desire. This longing is itself a gift of the Holy Spirit. It is the finger of the Holy Spirit that is writing the letter of God's word in us, and is helping us to recognize the whole range of oneself, a self that, of course, is given to rational and logical analysis and research, but which is also involved in an affective loving search.

Through the *anima* we enter into a better understanding of the mystery of God, who is love. Love, including God's love, is not only a capacity to produce reasonable, efficient, responsible actions with predictable results. Love is also the freedom in God. God is infinite vitality, constant inventiveness in love, absolute liberty. God loves each of us in a unique way, delights in hiding from us only to be found in greater depth. When we come to understand something of the mystery of God who is a Trinity of love, an infinite generosity and gift, an eternal play of love itself, then we will no longer be surprised to discover that sometimes God hides from us in order to make our heart's desire more acute and our joy more intense as we seek and find the Divine Lover again and again.

The young person whom I described as apparently near is the one who, imagining a God of static characteristics, thinks: God is this way and ought to act just so. But since God is not behaving as expected, something's wrong.

Do you recall Job's friends who, having just such an idea of God as static and rigidly coherent, concluded that Job had been wrong? But Job replied to them: I haven't been mistaken; I seek, and I continue to seek.

### Opening ourselves to "the more"

Entering into the dynamism of Trinitarian love corresponds to opening ourselves to the typology of the young person who "goes beyond." If I do not go beyond myself and beyond the horizons of daily life I touch very little of the mystery of God. This mystery is like a rushing mountain river which one understands only by throwing oneself right into it, allowing oneself to be borne along without fear by the cascading water. The mystery of God is a dynamism that we can understand only by opening ourselves to "the more."

Every time in our lives we open ourselves to the feeling of "more beyond" we feel contact, we experience God as near, and even if not near we continue to seek the divine One with an intensity that may be heroic. On the other hand, when we limit ourselves or want to make things overly precise, so to speak "closing the accounts," and establishing boundaries—this is allowable, this other thing is not—we are already in a narrow-minded mercantilism and God then disappears because that is not the divine way.

If therefore we think we have known the truth of God, but have not entered into the fire and playfulness of love, we are still actually somewhat distant from God.

The gift that the Lord wishes to offer us, and has always offered us in the Spirit, is the understanding that human beings realize themselves by going beyond themselves and giving themselves.

God does not exist except in the eternal relation of the gift of the Father to the Son, and this is unthinkable outside of the Spirit who is a continuous fountain of infinite love. The Spirit is the flame that burns without consuming, pure being on fire with love.

The prayer of adoration that we offer before the crucifix helps us in this journey into the knowledge of the divine mystery. There is no study of theology that corresponds to this growth in the experiential knowledge of God even if the *animus* in us seeks, by trying to coherently reorganize the data, some rational insight into the experience.

Without the factor of the *anima*—which Mary Magdalen evokes and which the passage from the Canticle of Canticles describes—there is no evangelical joy, and no authentic religious decision is taken.

In fact, every genuine spiritual growth requires that we go out of ourselves, that we let ourselves be taken hold of by God's dynamic love—better, by God who is love itself. Every spiritual realization requires the persevering search for that Love we have caught glimpses of.

We oughtn't be afraid therefore of seeking "him whom my heart loves," even if we do not find him. The seeking causes us to go out of ourselves, and sooner or later we will catch a glimmer of that One, we will catch hold of that fringe of Christ's tunic that is enough to support and heal us, to give us the courage and enthusiasm to conquer our pettiness.

The gospel passage that was read today (John 20:1, 11-18) ends with a shout of joy from Mary Magdalen: "I have seen the Lord!"

You are among those who can say you have seen the Lord, have seen something greater than yourselves, have been surprised by those supreme coordinates, the Lord's mercy and love. Jacob, too, had to admit: I was seeking who-knows-what, and then I saw the Lord.

Let us ask, through the intercession of the saint whom we commemorate today, that we allow ourselves to be moved by the Holy Spirit and that we may always live in an ever deeper seeking of God.

# Jacob Sets Out

*Lord, you who are always with us, today, tomorrow, in the days and years to come, do not let me have a disheartening fear of "after the retreat," do not let me be afraid of the banality of daily life that I will have to face again, of the lack of understanding from other people, of the whirlpool of all the distractions which might remove from my mind and heart the things that I have experienced in this retreat. May I learn from any temptation seeking to destroy my rule of life a greater awareness of you and of myself, and therefore a greater faith and a greater love. Mary, Mother of perseverance, help me not to underestimate this temptation but to look it squarely in the face, just as we ought to look openly at all the realities of life and death.*

Our present meditation will consist of two parts: the first refers to *Jacob setting out,* and the second I will call *Myself after the retreat.*

### Jacob sets out

So, Jacob has prayed; he has set up the memorial stone and anointed it; and he has made his vow. Now he sets out again on his journey.

Let us imagine ourselves asking Jacob: what has changed outwardly after the dream, the vision, the worshipful remembrance of the Lord?

I believe Jacob would have been able to say to us: in a certain sense nothing has changed. I have no more money in my pocket than I had before. I have no more food or supplies in my knapsack than before. The road I am to take is just as long as it was last night and it's still full of the unknown. I do not know whom I will meet on the way; maybe I will come across thieves and other evildoers. I don't know if Laban will receive me or refuse to open his doors to someone who has run away from home. So my future is just as uncertain as it was yesterday. Nonetheless, something has changed inside me.

Let us look at some of the things that have changed in and with respect to Jacob.

First of all, there is the *memorial*, the rock placed on end and anointed with oil. That remains where he put it. It is an undeniable fact to which Jacob will often refer, as can be read in the following chapters of the Book of Genesis.

Besides, along with the memorial, there is the *memory*, the conserving in his heart of that which he has seen and heard, and such a memory is a formidable interior force.

This memory constitutes a *new interpretive horizon*. The evening before, Jacob was dealing with asphyxiating points of reference, with constricting interpretive elements that gave him no room to breathe. But after his night's experience his frame of reference has been enlarged. What happened to him is what in Christian terminology is called *conversion*. Conversion is in fact a change in interpretive horizon that enables us to go forward in life in a new way.

So, Jacob departs, and we can imagine that he sets out on the road singing because he is full of hope, confidence, enthusiasm, and joy no longer with a fear of failure, without bitterness or a sense of frustration.

Finally, Jacob leaves in the certainty that *God is faithful*. He cannot be sure of his own faithfulness, nor presume that his enthusiasm and joy will last indefinitely, but he is certain of God's fidelity. This new awareness is very fundamental, and Satan tries continually to undermine this sort of awareness in

all of us because the Evil One cannot accept human beings en-
trusting themselves to the Lord once and for all. Jacob has understood God's faithfulness, and it is this above all that renews
his heart and his life.

It is lovely to read the story of Jacob's life as it unfolds after
the night of his dream, to see how he is accompanied by the
faithful love of God who continually recalls him to the experience of that night. The Bible shows us that in fact Jacob
did not change a lot inwardly right away, that morally he
managed only a gradual change. At bottom, he is still a bit of
a conniver, and his tendency to turn circumstances in his favor remains. For our part, after having made many good resolutions, we notice that our habits are about what they were
before. Nevertheless, what remains is the faithfulness of God,
whose work in us is mysterious and whose timetable is different from ours.

If we do not understand that God's faithfulness changes
us little by little, we risk—after we are involved in a new life—
having many delusions, becoming angry with ourselves, being discouraged. Since we are what we are, since our personal
history is a long one of frequent failure and our body is often
weighted down with the wounds of our life, it is essential to
let ourselves be enveloped by the faithful God who, slowly
or quickly, according to our life circumstances, changes us,
without our having the sensitivity to see it.

I suggest that we look at some further passages in the story
of Jacob. These narratives are rich with strange and surprising happenings, and each of them is punctuated with the repeated summons of the faithful Lord.

1. *Genesis 31*—After having made a fortune with Laban,
"Jacob learned that Laban's sons were saying, 'Jacob has taken
everything that belonged to our father, and he has accumu-
lated all this wealth of his by using our father's property.' "
(He is envied because his affairs are going well.) "Jacob per-
ceived, too, that Laban's attitude toward him was not what
it had previously been. Then the Lord said to Jacob, 'Return

to the land of your fathers, where you were born, and I will be with you' '' (vv. 1-3). In this new misadventure, caused in part by Jacob himself and in part by others' baseness, the Lord's fidelity is still present, and the trial becomes the occasion for returning to the land promised by God.

A little further on the memorial is recalled: "I am the God who appeared to you in Bethel, where you anointed a memorial stone and made a vow to me. Up, then! Leave this land and return to the land of your birth" (v. 13). The Lord remembered Jacob's memorial and will also remember you and these days of our retreat here and will always be ready to say to you: I am the One to whom you prayed in the retreat at Ballabio, to whom you promised one thing and another. I am with you!

2. In the following chapter of Genesis, chapter 32, we see how Jacob has to face, upon his return home, the unknown factor of his brother Esau, who fourteen years earlier had wanted to kill him. He does not know how the meeting with Esau will go, and he is full of discomfort and fear.

Sometimes it also happens to us that, returning to our neighborhood or district after having been gone for a long time, we wonder: Will I be accepted, will they understand me? Jacob himself survives this experience, even though things start out badly:

> When the messengers returned to Jacob, they said, ''We reached your brother Esau. He is now coming to meet you, accompanied by four hundred men.'' Jacob was very much frightened. In his anxiety, he divided the people who were with him, as well as his flocks, herds, and camels, into two camps. ''If Esau should attack and overwhelm one camp,'' he reasoned, ''the remaining camp may still survive.'' [Evidently, Jacob does not want to fight against his brother. He intends to meet him unarmed; but since Esau may be intent upon killing, Jacob divides his people and chattel, figuring that some will thereby escape death.] Then he prayed: ''O God of my father Abraham and God of my father Isaac! You told me, O Lord, 'Go back to the land of your birth, and I will be good to you.' I am un-

worthy of all the acts of kindness that you have loyally performed for your servant: although I crossed the Jordan here with nothing but my staff,'' [remember the extreme poverty of that original journey] ''I have now grown into two companies. Save me, I pray, from the hand of my brother Esau! Otherwise I fear that when he comes he will strike me down and slay the mothers and children. You yourself said, 'I will be very good to you, and I will make your descendants like the sands of the sea, which are too numerous to count.' Jacob then passed the night there'' (Gen 32:7-14a).

One might suppose that Jacob spent the night in prayer and that from that prayer came forth not only a deeper faith but also a little political and diplomatic ''know-how.'' ''Jacob selected from what he had with him presents for his brother Esau'' (v. 14b). While continuing to be unarmed, he wants to conquer Esau's heart. And so he prepares all possible gifts, charging his servants to carry them before him, his wives and children, and slaves.

And then comes the most mysterious and dramatic moment in Jacob's life:

In the course of that, Jacob arose, took his two wives, with the two maidservants and his eleven children, and crossed the ford of the Jabbok. After he had taken them across the stream and had brought over all his possessions, Jacob was left there alone. Then some man wrestled with him until the break of dawn. When the man saw that he could not prevail over him, he struck Jacob's hip at its socket, so that the hip socket was wrenched as they wrestled. The man then said, ''Let me go, for it is daybreak.'' But Jacob said, ''I will not let you go until you bless me.'' ''What is your name?'' the man asked. He answered, ''Jacob.'' Then the man said, ''You shall no longer be spoken of as Jacob, but as Israel, because you have contended with divine and human beings and have prevailed.'' Jacob then asked him, ''Do tell me your name, please.'' He answered, ''Why should you want to know my name?'' With that, he bade him farewell. Jacob named the place Peniel, ''Because I have seen God face to face,'' he said, ''yet my life has been spared'' (Gen 32:23-31).

The first vision—in which God was revealed as faithful—is not enough. The moment comes when, mysteriously (the passage is full of archaic popular elements difficult to interpret, but its basic meaning is clear enough), God and the human being wrestle with each other.

Saint Paul speaks of battling in prayer, and we also experience times in which prayer is a struggle and an agony, like that of Jesus' prayer in the Garden. It is difficult for me to say more about this passage that has inspired many mystics, persons living in great intimacy with God, who have recognized themselves in this story of Jacob's night of struggle and have understood that the faithfulness of the Lord can cause a dark night and a terrible battle in which one reaches the point where all we can do is ask for the divine blessing.

There comes to mind a book translated into Italian two years ago that is the interesting diary of a young woman who was a Dutch Jew. Believing in nothing, without any religious principle, she recounts with absolute lucidity going through psychoanalytic therapy, falling in love with her psychoanalyst, and the state of confusion she was in. Little by little, a great sense of God is given to her and she is irresistably caught up in the divine mystery.

The most extraordinary thing about her story is the fact that the last months of her life were spent in the deepest intimacy with God, so much so that she succeeds in describing serenely the Nazi persecution of the Jews. While the circle draws tighter around her and her family and friends she never expresses a word of contempt or bitterness. She is even able to write: We ought to endure all this with love, loving those who are destroying us.

Etty—the name of this young Jewish woman—confesses to being content and at peace even in the concentration camps, where she finds moments to pray, to adore God, to write in her diary—which she will entrust to a friend before being deported to Auschwitz, where she will go to her death with joy.

Hers is a mysterious story because it shows how the Lord can enter a totally irregular life and transform it, can illuminate an apparently closed and darkened situation.

Among Etty's recounted experiences I was also especially struck by her first encounter with the psychoanalyst, who before beginning the process of analysis, suggested that for the sake of the patient the two of them actually engage in something of a physical fight.

The Lord also wants to be involved in a mysterious struggle with us, a struggle such as that which caused Jacob to become a mature human being before God. That battle with the Lord enabled Jacob to vow never thereafter to avoid wrestling with God and to recognize the divine presence in the most dramatic moments of his life, including the most difficult, as, for example, when it seems as though he will never see his son Joseph again.

3. *Finally*, Genesis 35. Jacob, after many years, returns where his spiritual journey had begun, at Bethel, and fulfills his vow.

> God said to Jacob: "Go up now to Bethel. Settle there and build an altar there to the God who appeared to you while you were fleeing from your brother Esau." So Jacob told his family and all the others who were with him: "Get rid of the foreign gods that you have among you; then purify yourselves and put on fresh clothes. We are now to go up to Bethel, and I will build an altar there to the God who answered me in my hour of distress and who has been with me wherever I have gone" (vv. 1-3). [Having reached Bethel they build the altar,] for it was there that God had revealed himself to Jacob when he was fleeing from his brother (v. 7b). [And] On Jacob's arrival from Paddanaram, God appeared to him again and blessed him. God said to him: "You whose name is Jacob shall no longer be called Jacob, but Israel shall be your name. . . . I am God Almighty; be fruitful and multiply. A nation, indeed an assembly of nations, shall stem from you, and kings shall issue from your loins. The land I once gave to Abraham and Isaac I now give to you; and to your descendants after you will I give this land." Then

God departed from him. On the site where God had spoken with him, Jacob set up a memorial stone, and upon it he made a libation and poured out oil. Jacob named the site Bethel, because God had spoken with him there (vv. 9-15).

After many years and many twists and turns in his life, Jacob carried out his faithful promise to God. He had begun his journey in fear, had continued it in hope, and ever after bound himself to the One who had spoken to him.

### Myself after the retreat

On the heels of our reflections about Jacob let us try to focus on our own situation.

1. Of course when we go home each of us might say to himself/herself: Nothing has changed around me. I've had a very nice experience, with many insights; but no one will really notice anything different about me. I am settling in again at home and in my own little prayer nook in the house. I'm dealing again with the incessant television; I really ought to come up with a proper balance in my use of it, but that isn't easy.

And even I am not changed. My habits haven't changed, and probably I will once again fall into inertia, depressions, discouragements. Maybe I have deluded myself. Did the Lord help me or not during the retreat? Did God really say something to me then?

We have to accept all such difficulties and doubts, all such self-questioning since it is in the midst of all that that the Spirit of God mysteriously works.

2. Nevertheless, something has certainly changed, and it has changed to the degree in which we have been able during the retreat to pray and to know the Lord better.

First of all, *the interpretive horizon* has changed, and we oughtn't for all the world give up on this new horizon of our conversion, or better, this moment in the ongoing conversion in our life. In this new interpretive horizon the visible, tangible things of life are understood in connection with the invisible points of reference and with that fundamental coordinate that is God's faithful love.

And then there are the little *signs* of this change: *the rule of life*, which I carry with me; *Sacred Scripture*, which I have learned to read better and love more; *the Eucharist*, which abides in me and that I can re-discover every day; *prayer*; and the *memory* of what I have lived through in the retreat.

I have to take hold of and enter more deeply into these signs of change and be faithful to the resolutions made, so as not to allow the Enemy to get the upper hand. Otherwise, I will end up falling into trivializing activities and an undisciplined life.

3. Above all, *God is faithful*, and in prayer we are invited to become more and more profoundly certain of this. "You, Lord, are faithful, while I am or at least am able to be unfaithful. You, however, are not afraid of my infidelity because you are greater than I."

Then it will be easy to act because we will know that it is the Lord who is acting in us.

Fidelity to my resolutions is important only if it arises from my fidelity to God, who, reckoning with both my gifts and my limits, is building a home and a future for my heart and soul.

We must therefore keep in our heart the certitude of God's faithfulness, knowing that the root of every justification is not our good works, our noble efforts to do well (as essential as these are), but simply faith. God is the God of faith, and should be known as such.

In order to understand this truth better, let us read from the Letter to the Hebrews, where the patriarchs are spoken of:

> Faith is confident assurance concerning what we hope for, and conviction about things we do not see. Because of faith the men of old were approved by God. Through faith we perceive that the worlds were created by the word of God, and that what

is visible came into being through the invisible. By faith Abel offered God a sacrifice greater than Cain's. Because of this he was attested to be just, God himself having borne witness to him on account of his gifts; therefore, although Abel is dead, he still speaks. By faith Enoch was taken away without dying, and "he was seen no more because God took him." Scripture testifies that, before he was taken up, he was pleasing to God— but without faith, it is impossible to please him. . . . By faith Noah, warned about things not yet seen, revered God and built an ark that his household might be saved. He thereby condemned the world and inherited the justice which comes through faith. By faith Abraham obeyed when he was called, and went forth to the place he was to receive as a heritage; he went forth, moreover, not knowing where he was going (11:1-8).

And further on we find Jacob again recalling God: "By faith Jacob, when dying, blessed each of the sons of Joseph, and worshipped God, leaning on the head of his staff" (v. 21). It seems curious that the death of the man is described like this, especially since the Book of Genesis says simply that Jacob "leaned at the head of the bed" (Gen 47:31). Probably the staff that is mentioned by the author of the Letter to the Hebrews is the one with which Jacob had forded the Jabbok. It was therefore a memorial of what he had experienced—God's faithfulness—and he held it in his hand until his last breath, as if to show that the Lord had been faithful to him and he himself always held onto that certainty. But in the wood of the staff we can also see a symbol of the Cross. When we hold it in our hands, when we contemplate the crucifix, we have with us a visible sign of the Lord's love.

Chapter eleven of the Letter to the Hebrews continues by recalling a succession of patriarchs and their acts of faith; and then, in chapter twelve, it speaks of Jesus and ourselves: "Therefore, since we for our part are surrounded by this cloud of witnesses, let us lay aside every encumbrance of sin which clings to us and persevere in running the race which lies ahead; let us keep our eyes fixed on Jesus, who inspires and perfects our faith. For the sake of the joy which lay before him he endured the cross, heedless of its shame. He has taken his seat at the right hand of the throne of God. Remember how he endured the opposition of sinners; hence do not grow despondent or abandon the struggle" (Heb 12:1-3). Our task is to confront the future without illusions, without thinking that everything will be different, with the certainty that God's fidelity will bring us to where we should be, will enable us to attain the goals that the heart of God has decided for us, and that we, in this retreat, have placed in the heart of divine love.

### Expanding our horizons

With a reflection that seems to me particularly important we shall conclude our meditations. I express it by saying that we ought to enlarge our horizons, accepting the invitation that comes to us in the words with which the Lord promises Jacob: "In you and your descendants all the nations of the earth shall find blessing" (Gen 28:14b).

Jacob is not blessed only for his own sake, for his journey, for his entire life, brief or extended as that may be. He is blessed in view of the whole world. Justly, *The Jerusalem Bible* refers in this connection to the very similar words which God said to Abraham: "I will bless those who bless you and curse those who curse you. All the communities of the earth shall find blessing in you" (Gen 12:3). On this latter passage from Genesis *The Jerusalem Bible* notes: "The formula is repeated with the word 'family' or 'nation' in 18:18; 22:18; 26:4; 28:14. Its precise meaning is 'the nations shall say to each other: May you be blessed as Abraham was'" (cf. *The Jerusalem Bible*, p. 29). Abraham will be deemed so fortunate that even today you find people who will say when meeting someone who is enjoying luck: You are blessed like Abraham was!

Nevertheless, this formula, constantly repeated in Scripture, is enlarged in its significance, and the Book of Sirach, recalling the promises goes so far as to say: "God placed on the head of Jacob the promise and blessing for all peoples" (Sir 44:22). Such a blessing is the same that is seen again in the New Testament concerning Jesus: "You [said Peter speaking to the crowd in Jerusalem] are the children of those prophets, you are the heirs of the covenant God made with your fathers when he said to Abraham, 'In your offspring, all the families of the earth shall be blessed.' When God raised up his servant, he sent him to you first to bless you by turning you from your evil ways" (Acts 3:25-26). In the descent of Abraham and Jacob, that is, in Jesus, all the families of the earth will be blessed.

Saint Paul has the same interpretation: "Because Scripture saw in advance that God's way of justifying the Gentiles would be through faith, it foretold this good news to Abraham: 'All nations shall be blessed in you.' Thus it is that all who believe are blessed along with Abraham, the man of faith" (Gal 3:8-9).

There is a universal extension, in Jesus, of the blessing given to our fathers in the faith. All who were blessed were ultimately blessed *in Jesus*.

You, dear young people, ought therefore to extend your sights to the ends of the earth. Retreats can produce bad effects when the retreatant keeps everything for the self, perhaps coming up with a personal ideal of life which, however, cannot be realized precisely because it is too restricted.

So let us enlarge our horizons. We are people of the Church, in the Church, for the Church, and everything that we are we are as part of a humanity called to become Church, giving praise to God.

Therefore, in Abraham, in Jacob, in Jesus all humanity is blessed, and I am blessed and called for the sake of all humanity. Even if I were in fact to remain throughout my life in a very restricted space, if I live in a Christ-like way, I live for the whole world. Many great saints of the ages, and contemporary mystics like Saint Therese of the Child Jesus and Charles de Foucauld, lived their simple daily lives, with their ordinary activities, like this.

Let us therefore feel ourselves seriously co-responsible for the entire Church and for all men and women in the world. To this end, I invite you to re-read two contemporary Church documents. The first is the Second Vatican Council's Dogmatic Constitution on the Church, *Lumen Gentium*. It will help to expand the horizons of your mind and heart. In one respect at least, you belong to a less fortunate generation than mine, because for me the Council was an amazing event which I lived day after day. I still recall vividly the enthusiasm of those years when the conciliar Fathers were preparing the documents. Nonetheless, you ought to let yourselves be inspired by that great event of our century and obtain, from *Lumen Gentium*, for example, a true sense of the Church.

The second work that I suggest you attentively re-read is the recent encyclical of John Paul II, *Sollicitudo rei socialis*. This work shows how all human beings are interdependent and how necessary mutual solidarity is. The words of the Pope call us to extend our service to embrace all of humanity, and his summons will be very helpful to you in faithfully living in and loving God not in small doses and at minimal levels but with your heart free to race towards the future the Lord is preparing for you.

# Towards the Future

Homily for the sixteenth Sunday of the year
Liturgical texts: Genesis 18:1-10; Colossians 1:24-28; Luke 10:38-42

The gospel page for this Sunday somewhat describes the significance of the work we have accomplished during these days together. The passage from Genesis speaks to us of the results we have obtained, while the selection from Saint Paul's Letter to the Colossians opens us to the future.

## The better part that will not be taken away

Martha is a practical woman who lives everyday life with all its problems, and she doesn't much understand her sister Mary, who sits at the feet of Jesus listening to him. Martha gives voice to the thought of all those people whom we will meet tomorrow and in the near future who may ask us: What have you actually accomplished on your retreat? Why did you waste time with all that when there are so many other things to do and that need to be done?

It's often hard to really understand the importance of sitting at the feet of the Lord, and it is useless to try to explain it to scoffers. We just have to accept not being understood by everybody and to take heart from Jesus' words absolutely affirming that "Mary has chosen the better portion and she shall not be deprived of it" (Luke 10:42).

I hope you will return to your homes with the assurance that you have chosen the true and proper part, even if this assurance is constantly put in question and put to the test. Of course, duties, work, toil await you, but it remains true: your choice was correct.

And it is necessary that Jesus reminds us of our proper decision to come on retreat since we are sometimes confused and we think that perhaps it wasn't worth the pain of it, that nothing of the experience remains in us. At Bethany, Mary adored God, affirmed the primacy of the Word, and it doesn't matter if it *appears* that nothing of her action remains.

I pray and I shall continue to pray that you always have the strength to hold tight to this principle, of believing in Jesus more than in Martha, in the conviction that the centrality of God is recognized first of all in silent adoration and prolonged prayer. We labor in vain if our work does not have its roots in Mary's attitude.

### The outcome of the retreat

The text from Genesis (18:1-10) helps us to understand the results of our retreat. We have heard a splendid page: Abraham is rich, a man of means; he does not receive the wayfarer with condescension but all but thanks him for the opportunity to do him a service.

"The Lord appeared to Abraham by the terebinth of Mamre, as he sat in the entrance of his tent, while the day was growing hot. Looking up, he saw three men standing nearby." Note that Abraham doesn't know who these men are and he probably takes them to be paupers. "When he saw them, he ran from the entrance of the tent to greet them; and bowing to the ground, he said, 'Sir, if I may ask you this favor, please do not go on past your servant. Let some water be brought, that you may bathe your feet, and then rest yourselves under the tree. Now that you have come this close to your servant, let me bring you a little food, that you may refresh yourselves; and afterward you may go on your way.' 'Very well,' they replied, 'do as you have said.' ''

Abraham does not wait for the strangers to ask for hospitality but runs to greet them and bows down to them. Such is the marvelous welcoming that we still find today among many peoples, perhaps more often in the southern regions of the globe than in the north. I recall arriving once in a very poor African hut where the people asked nothing more than to be of service, taking the bread from their own plates and giving it to the person who had just come in; and all this with no fuss or fanfare at all.

Similarly, Abraham not only did a good thing but did it in a very gentle and unpretentious way. We see that he was then rewarded beyond his imagination, for what was said to him was not a simple ''Thank you'' but something extraordinary and wonderful: '' 'Where is your wife Sarah?' they asked him. 'There in the tent,' he replied. One of them said, 'I will surely return to you about this time next year, and Sarah will then have a son.' ''

Abraham's humility brings a superabundant fulfillment. His attitude is like the Virgin Mary's. She, receiving the visit from the angel, was full of awe, of humility, without presumption, as one who didn't make much of herself and wouldn't think of asking for much. And then she is filled with gifts, including the Gift without equal.

The Lord has granted us a somewhat similar experience. You have been listening to the Lord without presumption, without seeking the spectacular achievements in the limelight which vanity suggests, but with openness and availability, with willingness, with the confidence of one who does not feel important but is happy to be able to offer a small service to the Lord.

And I am certain that Jesus has a word, a promise for each one of you, like that promise the Lord made first to Abraham and then to Jacob. I am sure that the Lord intends your life to be a truly rich and fruitful human life, one beyond your ability to imagine.

If I look back upon myself at your age, taking part in a retreat like this, and then I see how much the Lord has accomplished in me, I am forced to recognize the total disproportion between the very little service I managed to give God—in practical works as well as in adoration and in seeking the Lord in Scripture—and what has happened in me.

The Lord is great with each of us, in visible ways but especially in invisible ones, repaying faithful lives one hundredfold.

The same goes for the service I have tried to offer you, in order to help you and put you at your ease in prayer and in reading Scripture. Like Abraham I went as it were to bring you a little water, to wash your feet and make you comfortable under the tree, knowing well my incapacity. Nonetheless, you have already given back much to me, because I have been able to contemplate, in the words of the Apostle Paul, ''Christ in you, your hope of glory'' (Col 1:27).

## Towards the future

My last reflection is on the Letter to the Colossians where it says: ''Even now I find my joy in the suffering I endure for you. In my own flesh I fill up what is lacking in the sufferings of Christ for the sake of his body, the church'' (Col 1:24).

During our time together here we have become more clearly aware of our limits, of our difficulties and sufferings, of our moments of desolation, aridity, weariness, and darkness, of our times of being lost and at sea. But the sufferings that we endure are nothing if they are not a symbol of and a small participation in the sufferings of the Church and the world.

We must learn to read our moments of obscurity as part of the darkness of many who are believers and baptized; our disheartening moments as part of the discouragements the Church endures, that young persecuted Christians suffer, and that missionaries living in the midst of hostile people must bear.

Sufferings will not be lacking us in the future, and the apostle invites us to see them as a gift from the Lord, who wants us to experience in our own body and person something of what the Church experiences in her entirety.

It is part of the invitation to think and feel daily with the Church in every situation in our life, to do so in dealing with our weaknesses, incapacities, and regrets, even our sins; to suffer with and for the Church, for the benefit of the Body of Christ, to which in some manner we are all committed.

Paul, in the Letter to the Colossians, speaks of "the mission that God has entrusted to me on your behalf" (v. 25). In fact, we have all entered into this mission. No matter what your vocation will be, no one need ever take from your heart the certainty that life is a gift to spend in union with the whole Church for the sake of others. In this way you will be able to face in a new light the difficulties and obstacles you encounter.

*Lord, your word is truth, and we ask you to consecrate us in your love. We commit ourselves to you, knowing we are weak and fragile. Perhaps there will be days when it will seem to us that we no longer retain anything of value from this retreat. But you are faithful and you have placed us on a journey of solidarity with the whole Church and all of humanity, a journey that you will bring to fulfillment according to your promise. With this faith and confidence we do not fear the future; rather, we ready ourselves for it with joy.*

The act of placing your hand on the gospel—which you will be doing after the prayer of the faithful—and the kiss of peace, by which you embrace the Church, will be symbols of your trust in God's fidelity and in the Word of the Lord which is truth and which consecrates you in the divine love.

*Also by Carlo-Maria Martini*

# In the Thick of His Ministry

Cardinal Martini, reflecting on some passages of the second letter to the Corinthians, delves deeply into Paul. Here "we find Paul in the thick of his ministry. After twenty years of it, during which he passed through so many trials, disappointments and difficulties, he speaks as a servant of the gospel in the midst of the daily grind. So we feel he is very close to us."

The Cardinal then draws an accurate portrait of the pastor serving the gospel in faith today. We are shown the richness and possibilities of this life "even though some days may be beset with sufferings and misunderstandings." It is devotion to the Word that shapes the daily service to the community, providing the minister with previously unimagined goals.

Though initially intended for young priests working in diverse pastoral situations, *In the Thick of His Ministry* is for anyone committed to the service of the gospel.

**1995-9 Paper, 91 pp., 5 3/8 x 8 1/2**
Rights: U.S. and Canada

Available at your religious bookstore or from

THE LITURGICAL PRESS
St. John's Abbey, P.O. Box 7500
Collegeville, MN 56321-7500
Phone: 612-363-2213     Fax: 1-800-445-5899